GOLF

BY MICHAEL V. USCHAN

Lucent Books, Inc.
San Diego, California

Titles in The History of Sports Series include:
Baseball
Basketball
Football
Golf
Hockey
Soccer

For putting up with my on-course misadventures and endless philosophizing about the game I love, I dedicate this book to Mike Bates and Mary Kuta, Bill Dormin, Van Johnson, Jack Kelvie, and Greg Radke.

On cover: Golfing legend Bobby Jones.

Library of Congress Cataloging–in–Publication Data

Uschan, Michael V., 1948–
    Golf / by Michael V. Uschan.
        p.   cm. — (History of sports)
    Includes bibliographical references and index.
    Summary: Discusses the origins and evolution of the game of golf including memorable events, key personalities, and the game's history.
    ISBN 1-56006-744-6
    1. Golf—History—Juvenile literature. [1. Golf—History.] I. Title. II. Series.
    GV968 .U83   2001
    796.352—dc21   00-009159

Copyright © 2001 by Lucent Books, Inc.
P.O. Box 289011, San Diego, CA 92198-9011
Printed in the U.S.A.

Contents

FOREWORD

MORE THAN MANY areas of human endeavor, sports give us the opportunity to see the possibilities in our physical selves. As participants, we all too quickly find limits in how fast we can run, how high we can jump, how far and straight we can hit a golf ball. But as spectators we can surpass those limits as we view the accomplishments of others and see how fast, how smooth, and how strong a human being can be. We marvel at the gravity-defying leaps of a Michael Jordan as he strains towards a basketball hoop or at the dribbling of a Mia Hamm as she eludes defenders on the soccer field. We shake our heads in disbelief at the talents of a young Tiger Woods hitting an approach shot to the green or the speed of a Carl Lewis as he appears to glide around an Olympic track.

These are what the sports media call "the oohs and ahhs" of sports—the stuff of highlight reels and *Sports Illustrated* covers. But to understand a sport only in the context of its most artistic modern athletes is shortsighted, for it does little justice to the accomplishments of the athlete *or* to the sport itself. Far more wise is to view a sport as a continuum—a constantly moving, evolving process. On this continuum are not only the superstars of today, but the people who first played the sport, who thought about rules and strategies that would make it more challenging to play as well as a delight to watch.

Lucent Books' series, *The History of Sports,* provides such a continuum. Each book explores the development of a sport, from its basic roots onwards, and tries to answer questions that a reader might wonder about. Who were its first players and what sorts of rules did the sport have then? What kinds of equipment were used in the beginning and what changes have taken place over the years?

Each title in *The History of Sports* also identifies key individuals in the sport's history—people whose leadership or skills have made a difference in the way the sport is played today. Included will be the easily recognized names, the Mia Hamms and the Sammy Sosas, the Wilt Chamberlains and the Wilma Rudolphs. But there are also the names of past greats, people like baseball's King Kelly, soccer's Sir Stanley Matthews, and basketball's Hank Luisetti—who may be less familiar today, but were as synonymous with their sports at one time as the "oohs and ahhs" players of today.

Finally, the series looks at the aspects of a sport that are particularly important in its current point on the continuum. Baseball today is better understood knowing about salary caps and union negotiators. One cannot truly know modern soccer without knowing about the specter of fan violence at matches. And learning about the role of instant replay is critical to a thorough understanding of today's professional football games. In viewing a sport as a continuum, the strides that have been made along the way are that much more admirable. It is a richer view, and one that shows how yesterday's limits have been surpassed—and how the limits of today are the possibilities of athletes in the future.

An Ancient Game Gathers Strength for a New Millennium

Aᴿɴᴏʟᴅ Pᴀʟᴍᴇʀ ɪꜱ one of the most revered golfers of all time, the daring player who in the 1960s excited throngs of cheering fans known as "Arnie's Army" to ignite a new era of popularity for golf. Palmer, who loves the sport itself more than the fame and riches it has brought him, sums up the game as well as anyone ever has:

> Golf is deceptively simple and end-lessly complicated. A child can play it well and a grown man can never master it. Any single round of it is full of unex-pected triumphs and perfect shots that end in disaster. It is almost a science, yet it is a puzzle without an answer. It is gratifying and tantalizing, precise and unpredictable; it requires complete con-centration and total relaxation. It satis-fies the soul and frustrates the intellect. It is at the same time rewarding and maddening—and it is without doubt the greatest game mankind has ever in-vented.[1]

As Palmer says, golf is "deceptively sim-ple." Players place a small white ball before them and keep hitting it with a variety of clubs until it falls, with a satisfying plop, into a small hole on a lush, manicured ex-panse of short-cut grass known as a green.

But as Palmer also notes, it is "endlessly complicated." Hitting a golf ball can be dif-ficult and frustrating. A mishit of fractions of an inch sends the ball veering far to the

Arnold Palmer, one of golf's most beloved champions, smiles after hitting his tee shot in a practice round for the 2000 Masters.

how hard the game is."[2] Yet as a new millennium dawned, this humbling, fascinating, infuriating game was more popular than at any time in history.

The Sport Evolves

Golf began in the 1400s on informally laid out courses along Scotland's rugged, windswept seacoast. British travelers carried the game to Canada, Australia, India, and other outposts of their country's worldwide empire, but the game did not take root in the United States until the late 1880s, when a Scottish immigrant named John Reid began playing in Yonkers, New York.

Ultimately, the twentieth century was the most important in golf's long history as well as the most transitional. Equipment evolved from wooden clubs and balls made from hardened tree sap to drivers and irons of exotic metals like titanium and high-tech balls that flew much farther. New machinery freed architects to sculpt the earth into any shape they desired, enabling them to create dramatic new courses with island holes surrounded by water or desert courses that were an oasis of green in a sea of sand and cactus.

target's left or right; a gently stroked putt rolls perfectly for thirty feet, only to stop a tantalizing quarter inch short of the hole; a long, straight, arcing drive flies one foot too far, landing in a sand trap to create a difficult second shot.

It is such a hard game to play well every day that even the best players sometimes struggle. Eldrick "Tiger" Woods, who entered the twenty-first century as the world's best golfer, freely admits: "Golf humbles you every day, every shot really. I know

The most important changes, however, were social ones that made the game accessible to more people. Once played only by royalty and the rich, today men, women, and children in many countries play golf. Players include people of many races and economic levels—from multimillionaires like basketball legend Michael Jordan to inner city boys and girls learning the game in cities across America. In the United States,

golf freed itself from its segregated past as minorities and women won their fight for acceptance.

Golfing on the Moon

The twentieth century even saw golf transported to the moon when Alan Shepard Jr.,

Although these young African Americans were learning to play golf in 1944, there were not many minority golfers until late in the twentieth century.

During the 1971 Apollo 14 mission, astronaut Alan Shepard Jr. (pictured here) became the first golfer in outer space.

commander of the *Apollo 14* space mission, took along a golf club with a specially constructed four-piece shaft. To honor the game he loved, while Shepard was on the moon in February 1971, he struck his way into golf history. He said,

> Just before climbing up the ladder [of the lunar module] to come home, I prepared to tee off! When I dropped the first ball, it took about three seconds to land, and bounced a couple of times in the gray dust. I made my best slow-motion, one-handed half-swing. Making a full swing in a space suit is impossible. I made good contact and the ball, which would have gone thirty to forty yards on Earth, went over 200 yards. The ball stayed up in the black sky almost thirty seconds. I was so excited I swung harder on the second one, which I [mishit] about forty yards into a nearby crater! I decided to call that a hole-in-one, even if the hole was several miles in diameter.[3]

CHAPTER 1

The Early History of Golf

THE EXACT DATE and place golf was first played is unknown. Although Scotland is considered the game's true ancestral home, historians from several other nations claim that their own countries were the sport's true birthplace.

The problem in determining golf's origin, however, is that games whose object is to hit a small ball show up in several cultures. For example, the Romans played *paganica* in which they hit feather-stuffed balls with curved bats. In *chola,* the Belgians and French wielded iron clubs to knock a wooden ball to a goal in a cross-country event, one in which teams tried to stop each other from advancing. The Japanese played *dakyu* as early as the 700s and the Chinese *suigan* in the 1200s; both games utilized wooden balls and sticks slightly resembling golf clubs.

Scotland's strongest rival as golf's originator is Holland, where Dutch historian Steven Van Hengel claims *kolven* was played as early as 1297. However, English historian Robert Browning denies that early Dutch sport was a forerunner of golf:

> Kolven is not a field game at all, but is played in a covered space on a wooden floor or on kolf-courts such as are found attached to some inns. It is played with a club that does certainly resemble a clumsy golf club, but the balls are large and heavy—about the size of a cricket ball and a couple of pounds in weight. The object of the

game is to strike two posts set up from 40 to 80 feet apart at opposite ends of the court.[4]

Yet despite all the arguments to the contrary, most historians agree that golf's ancestry belongs to Scotland. As Herbert Warren Wind, America's finest golf writer, states unequivocally: "The Scots were the first to play a game in which the players used an assortment of clubs to strike a ball into a hole dug in the earth. This is the essence of the game we know as golf. It is generally accepted that golf is the product of Scotland."[5]

Golf's Scottish Origin

The first Scottish playing sites were sandy strips of land along the coast, areas called *linksland* or links because they were considered a link between the ocean and more fertile land used for agriculture. The name links survives as a generic term for any golf course. These common areas were free for anyone to use, had grass clipped short by grazing sheep, and contained sandy soil that drained quickly after rains. Many early courses were roughly laid out along high bluffs above the sea on sites with natural dunes, ridges, gullies, and hollows, physical features that still mark a true links-style course.

In *The Origin of Golf,* historian Sir W. G.

This humorous 1911 sketch symbolizes the game's Scottish origin.

Simpson in 1887 theorized about how the game began:

A shepherd tending his sheep would often chance upon a round pebble, and, having his crook in his hand, he would strike it away. But once on a time (probably) a shepherd feeding his sheep on a links—perhaps those of St. Andrews—rolled one of those stones into a rabbit [hole]. Our shepherd hailed another to witness his endeavor. "Forsooth, that is easy," said the friend, and trying failed.[6]

Golf's Scottish origin extends to the name of the sport itself, which is believed to have derived from the Scottish word *gouf*, meaning to strike. In its earliest years "golf" was spelled variously as *golfe, goff, gouff, goffe, gow'lf,* and *gowf.*

The Scots Play Golf

The first historical reference to golf was a March 6, 1457, edict from King James II of Scotland declaring "that futeball [soccer] and golfe be utterly cryed down [prohibited] and not used."[7] During that time, Scotland was at war with England and James was worried his soldiers were forsaking archery practice to play the two sports. Golf, however, remained wildly popular and survived two more attempts to bar it in 1471 and 1491. Finally, in 1502 when Scotland made peace with England, golf was again sanctioned in the country of its origin.

Golf became popular with Scottish royalty, including King James IV, King James V, and Mary, Queen of Scots—who, after ascending the Scottish throne in 1559, played at St. Andrews, the university town

King James II (left) tried to ban golf in 1457, but Scots loved the game so much they ignored his edict and kept playing.

Mary, Queen of Scots, was one of history's first women golfers. A crowd gathers to watch her hit a shot, possibly at the St. Andrews links.

that gave its name to the world's most famous golf course. Mary was one of the first women golfers, and her son, James VI of Scotland, took the game to England in 1608 when he ascended England's throne as King James I.

The game continued on an informal basis until 1744, when the Company of Gentlemen Golfers (later known as The Honourable Company of Edinburgh Golfers) started the world's first club devoted to the sport. The Company was organized because a governing body was needed to formalize rules for an annual tournament in which the Council of Edinburgh agreed to award a silver golf club to the victor. The rules were needed because prior to 1744 there was no standardization in how golf was played. The Company formulated thirteen basic regulations, several of which survive today including "He whose ball lyes farthest from the hole is obliged to play first."[8]

The Society of St. Andrews Golfers in St. Andrews, Scotland, began play a decade later. In 1834 King William IV of England granted the group his patronage, and it was renamed the Royal and Ancient Golf Club of St. Andrews. The club eventually became the governing body for golf worldwide, responsible for updating rules and maintaining the game's integrity. For example, at first there was no set number of holes a golf course had to have. But in 1764 St. Andrews reduced its course from 22 holes to 18, and its prestige was so great that 18 became the standard for the rest of the world.

Golf Travels the World

In 1608 James I carried the game to England when he played on Blackheath in London. In 1766 the Honourable Company of Golfers at Blackheath became the first club to exist outside Scotland. The sport grew slowly until the mid–nineteenth century, when golf spread throughout England, Ireland, and

THE FIRST RULES OF GOLF

In 1744 the Honourable Company of Edinburgh Golfers set down the first thirteen rules of golf. These original regulations are important because they shaped golf for all time by standardizing the way it was played. These original rules, translated into modern English from the archaic Scottish, are listed below. They are from Robert R. McCord's *Golf: An Album of Its History*.

1. You must tee your ball within a club-length of the hole.
2. Your tee must be upon the ground.
3. You are not to change the ball which you strike off the tee.
4. You are not to remove stones, bones or any break-club for the sake of playing your ball, except on the fair green, and that only within a club's length of your ball.
5. If your ball come among water or any watery filth, you are at liberty to take your ball and throw it behind the hazard six yards at least; you may play it with any club, and allow your adversary a stroke for so getting out your ball.
6. If your balls be found anywhere touching one another, you are to lift the first ball until you play the last.

7. At holing you are to play your ball honestly for the hole, and not to play upon your adversary's ball, not lying in your way to the hole.
8. If you should lose your ball by its being taken up or any other way, you are to go back to the spot where you struck last and drop another ball and allow your adversary a stroke for the misfortune.
9. No man at holing his ball is to be allowed to mark his way to the hole with his club or anything else.
10. If a ball be stop'd by any person, horse, dog, or anything else, the ball so stop'd must be played where it lyes.
11. If you draw your club in order to strike and proceed so far with your stroke as to be bringing down your club, if then your club shall break in any way, it is accounted as a stroke.
12. He who whose ball lyes farthest from the hole is obliged to play first.
13. Neither trench, ditch, or dyke made for the preservation of the links, nor the Scholar's Holes or the Soldier's Lines, shall be accounted a hazard, but the ball is to be taken out, teed, and play'd with any iron club.

Great Britain's colonies around the world. In 1800 the United Kingdom had only 7 golf clubs, a figure that grew to 34 by 1870, 387 two decades later, and 2,330 by 1900.

Historian David Stirk explains how the British spread the sport globally: "Scottish golfing enthusiasts sent by the great business houses of London or by the colonial service to every part of the empire and to other countries, took the game and their love of it with them."[9]

Built in 1829 by British army officers, the Royal Calcutta Golf Club in India was the first outside Great Britain. Royal Calcutta was followed by Royal Bombay (India) in 1842, Royal Adelaide (Australia) in 1871, Royal Cape (South Africa) in 1885, Royal Bangkok (Thailand) in 1890, Shanghai Golf Club (China) in 1896, and even a course on the slopes of Mount Rokko in Kobe, Japan, in 1903.

The Golf Club de Pau in France, the European continent's first, was built in 1856 at the request of Scottish soldiers convalescing there from injuries suffered in one of Great Britain's many battles with the French. The Royal Montreal Golf Club in Canada began play in 1873, making it North America's oldest continuously operating club.

Golf in America

A handful of British colonists, however, brought the game to the New World more than a century before Royal Montreal opened. Proof that the game slipped across the Atlantic Ocean in the eighteenth century is a document written in 1772 by Dr. Benjamin Rush, a historical figure famous for

A golfer prepares to sink a putt in a match at Blackheath in 1870. Players in this period wore formal attire, including ties.

ST. ANDREWS: GOLF'S ANCESTRAL, HONORED HOME

The clubhouse at the Royal and Ancient Golf Club of St. Andrews.

The Royal and Ancient Golf Club of St. Andrews is considered the sport's true home. Founded in 1754 as the Society of St. Andrews Golfers, the club's name was changed in 1834 when English King William IV granted it his favor. St. Andrews soon became the most prestigious club in Scotland and, eventually, the world. Its stature was so great that in 1764, when it reduced the length of its course from 22 holes to 18, that number was adopted worldwide as the standard for all courses.

The following account of how this happened is from *Golf Magazine's Encyclopedia of Golf:*

The course at St. Andrews—what would now be the famous Old Course—had twelve holes. The first eleven traveled straight out to the end of a small peninsula. After playing these, the golfers returned to the clubhouse by playing the first ten greens backward, plus a solitary green by the clubhouse. Thus a "round" of golf consisted of twenty-two holes. The outgoing holes were marked with a small iron pin with white flags, while the incoming holes were marked with a red flag [a tradition still observed today on courses around the world]. In 1764, however, the Royal and Ancient resolved that the first four holes should be converted into two. Since this change automatically converted the same four holes into two on the way back, the "round" was reduced from twenty-two holes to eighteen.

being a signer of the Declaration of Independence and surgeon general of the Continental army during the American Revolution.

A pamphlet Rush authored titled "Sermons to Gentlemen upon Temperance and Exercise" is the first American publication to mention golf. Rush even promoted the game as an excellent way for colonists to improve their health:

> Golf is an exercise which is much used by the Gentlemen of Scotland. A large common, in which there are several little holes, is chosen for the purpose. It is played with little leather balls stuffed with feathers; and sticks made somewhat in the form of a handy-wicket. He who puts a ball into a given number of holes, with the fewest strokes, gets the game. A man would live ten years the longer for using this exercise once or twice a week.[10]

Further evidence of the game's early colonial debut is the following advertisement from the April 21, 1779, edition of New York City's *Rivington Royal Gazette:* "To the golf players: The season for this pleasant and healthy exercise now advancing, gentlemen may be furnished with excellent clubs and the veritable Caledonian [Scottish] balls, by enquiring at the printer's."[11]

Scottish immigrants who settled around Charleston, South Carolina, and Savannah, Georgia, also brought their homeland's sport.

Copies of the *Charleston City Gazette* from the late 1700s indicate the South Carolina Golf Club was started there in 1786, and historical records show that golf was also played in Savannah during this period.

However, except for a few scattered players who informally pursued the game, golf died out in the United States until the late nineteenth century, partly due to the difficulty of getting equipment from Scotland, a result of America's war with Great Britain. But the sport would be revived in 1888 thanks to John Reid, "the father of American golf."

The Apple Tree Gang

Born in 1840 in Dunfermline, Scotland, Reid immigrated to America and became an executive with the J. L. Mott Iron Works in the New York City area. In 1887 when fellow Scot Robert Lockhart returned home for the Christmas holiday, Reid asked him to bring back some golf equipment so he could take up the game.

Lockhart purchased two dozen balls and six clubs (three woods and three irons) from Tom Morris, a legendary Scottish golf champion. On an unseasonably warm February 22, 1888, Reid and several friends created a makeshift course in a cow pasture adjoining his home in Yonkers. The following description of this historic round, considered the official birth of golf in the United States, is from Wind's *The Story of American Golf:*

Legendary golfer Tom Morris prepares to hit a shot in 1880.

yards long were laid out over the hilly ground, and "cups" were scooped out of the earth with [an iron]. There weren't enough clubs for everyone, so John B. Upham was selected to oppose Reid in this, the first game of golf to be played by the men who later formed the St. Andrew's Golf Club, the first permanent golf club in the United States. No scores were kept that morning [but] the two players and [several] spectators were in full agreement that golf was great fun, a game with a very bright future. Scotland could well be proud of itself.[12]

Reid and his friends—Upham, Harry Holbrook, Kingman H. Putnam, and Henry Tallmadge—ordered more equipment, moved to a thirty-acre pasture in April so they could create a larger 6-hole course, and played throughout the summer. On November 14 at a banquet to celebrate their athletic experiment, the small group decided to establish the St. Andrew's Golf Club, today the oldest continuously operating club in America. The name was chosen to honor the game's Scottish heritage, but in deference to the original St. Andrews an apostrophe was added.

Washington's birthday, 1888, was a wondrously mild day. Reid had originally planned to wait until late March or April before trying the clubs himself, but that twenty-second of February was the kind of a day that makes a man want to hurry the spring, and John Reid could wait no longer. He got in touch with [some friends] and buoyed with the sense of adventure, they crossed to the field Reid used as his cow pasture. Three short holes each about a hundred

In 1892 St. Andrew's moved to an even bigger tract that included an apple orchard,

ALMOST ARRESTED FOR PLAYING GOLF?

Golf histories throughout the decades have contained conflicting reports about whether Robert Lockhart was arrested for testing the clubs and balls he bought in Scotland for John Reid. But in *Golf in America*, George Peper clears up the lingering controversy by quoting an interview with Lockhart's son, Sydney, concerning the incident in a New York City park:

One bright Sunday morning, father, my brother Leslie, and myself went up to a place on the river, which is now Riverside Drive. Father teed up the first little white ball and, selecting one of the long wooden clubs, dispatched it far down the meadow. He tried all the clubs and then we boys were permitted to drive some balls too. One of father's shots came dangerously close to taking the ear off an iceman, but the mounted policeman [who was a spectator] did not arrest my father, and merely smiled. Later the cop asked if he could hit one of those balls and naturally my father was more than pleased. The officer got down off his horse and went through the motions of teeing up, aping [copying] father in waggling and squaring off to the ball and other preliminaries. Then he let go and hit a beauty straight down the field which went fully as far as any father had hit. Being greatly encouraged and proud of his natural ability, he tried again. This time he missed the ball completely and then in rapid succession he missed the little globe three more times; so with a look of disgust on his face he mounted his horse and rode away.

which historian George Peper says generated a nickname for these pioneer players:

It was here that the group became known as the Apple Tree Gang, the moniker referring to one tree in particular, which was situated near the first tee and final green and which served as a combination locker room and nineteenth hole [refreshment center]. In its branches the members hung their coats, their lunch baskets, and a wicker demijohn containing [drinks]. A wide wooden seat encircling the trunk served as the club's lounge.[13]

Golf Booms in America

Once Reid brought golf to America, the game spread quickly. In 1888 the only course was that 6-holer in Yonkers, but by 1896 there were more than 80, by 1900 over 1,000 (more than the rest of the world combined), by 1930 a total of 5,586, and at the end of the twentieth century more than 16,000. The game spread so quickly that in 1895 the *New York Times* commented: "In the history of American field sports there can be found no outdoor pastime that developed and attained such popularity in such a relatively short period of time as the game of golf."[14]

Many of the first courses were in eastern states—the Tuxedo (New York) Golf Club; Newport (Rhode Island) Country Club; Middlesboro (Kentucky) Country Club; the Country Club in Brookline, Massachusetts;

and Shinnecock Hills Golf Club on Long Island, New York. But in 1892 American-born Charles Blair Macdonald, who learned the game and studied Scottish courses while attending St. Andrews University, founded the Chicago Golf Club in Wheaton, Illinois. It only had 6 holes originally but within a few years Macdonald made it into the nation's first with 18 holes, the standard St. Andrews had set a century earlier.

In 1894 Macdonald had two chances to prove he was America's finest golfer, a reputation he had earned by winning almost every match he played. However, in September the Newport Country Club hosted a medal play tournament, and Macdonald lost by a stroke to Newport's William G. Lawrence, who shot 188 for 36 holes. That October Macdonald was beaten again in a match play event at St. Andrew's, falling to St. Andrew's member Laurence B. Stoddard.

Macdonald was a sore loser, but, in the end, something positive did result from his poor sportsmanship. Wind explains that it was Macdonald's complaints about the tournaments that led to the creation of the United States Golf Association (USGA):

> Macdonald refused to recognize Stoddard as the national champion. As he saw it, Stoddard had won a tournament, a tournament sponsored by one club. One club could not speak for a nation. Before a tournament could be the designated national championship, it would [need] the approval of all the clubs in the country, and those clubs would have to be joined in an official organization.[15]

In response to Macdonald's carping, delegates from five clubs—St. Andrew's, Newport, The Country Club (Brookline,

Founded in 1888, St. Andrew's Golf Club in Yonkers, New York, is the longest continuously operating golf club in the United States.

Massachusetts), Shinnecock Hills, and Chicago—met in New York on December 22, 1894, and agreed to establish a governing body for golf. They organized the Amateur Golf Association of the United States, a name later changed to the Amateur Golf Association and then the United States Golf Association, its current title.

Theodore Havemeyer was elected the group's first president. Known as the Sugar King for the fortune he made in that industry, Havemeyer donated $1,000 for the trophy for the first U.S. Amateur Championship at Newport in October 1895. In that tournament Macdonald won, beating Charles Sands in the 36-hole match play final to become the first official champion of all America. The inaugural U.S. Open for professional golfers was played at Newport the day after the Amateur ended. Englishman Horace Rawlins, Newport's assistant pro, won $150 in cash and a gold medal worth $50.

The first U.S. Women's Amateur Championship was also held that year. But the competitors, like female golfers in the rest of the world, were having as much trouble being accepted as equals on the golf course as they were in everyday life during an era in which male domination was generally accepted.

Early Women Golfers

In 1890, *Outing* magazine claimed golf was good for American women: "As a game for ladies, there can be no doubt that it must become a favorite and popular one. It has the advantage of giving plenty of moderate and healthful exercise, without any of that other exertion that tennis may call forth and which every young lady is not equal to."[16]

The tone of that article sounds chauvinistic today and reflects the negative attitude women golfers in those days had to overcome. Women in Great Britain and the United States were denied the right to play on many courses, forcing them to start their own clubs. The St. Andrews (Scotland) Ladies Golf Club in 1867 was the first, and by 1886 it had five hundred members.

Men derided women who were serious about golf and wanted to hold their own major competitions. In 1893 when the Ladies Golf Union organized the first British Ladies Championship at Royal Lytham and St. Anne's, a course near London, a British golf official sarcastically commented: "They will never go through *one* Ladies Championship with credit. Tears will bedew, if wigs do not bestrew, the green."[17] But the tournament went smoothly, and the first champion was Lady Margaret Scott, who also won the next two titles before retiring to marry and become Lady Margaret Hamilton-Russell.

The battle women had in gaining access to courses was shown by a group of women in Morristown, New Jersey, who in the spring of 1894 opened the 7-hole Morris County Golf Club because they were not allowed to play on other local courses. The

Some of the women golfers who helped pioneer the sport in America pose proudly in this photograph from the late 1800s.

women golfers, however, made the mistake of allowing two hundred men to join as associate members. By the following January a male had become president, and the men took over the club.

The only consolation for the Morristown women was that in 1896 the USGA held its second U.S. Women's Amateur Championship on their course, with sixteen-year-old Beatrix Hoyt winning the first of her three straight titles. The winner of the first amateur in 1895 at Meadow Brook Club in Hempstead, New York, had been Mrs. C. S. Brown of Shinnecock Hills, whose 132 total for 18 holes topped a dozen other players.

The World Loves Golf

The difficulty early golfers had in playing can be seen by the scores they recorded during those early championships. Brown's 132 total to win the first U.S. women's championship is 50 or more strokes higher than top players shoot today in similar competitions, and the men of Brown's era did not fare much better.

Despite the fact that golf is a tough game to play well, it caught on wherever it was taken. From Australia to America, France to Fiji, Japan to Jamaica, it stands today as the single greatest cultural export Scotland has ever produced.

CHAPTER 2

The Basics of the Game

MARK TWAIN, WHO penned the American classics *Tom Sawyer* and *Huckleberry Finn,* once offered the unflattering opinion that golf is "a good walk spoiled."[18] Like many people, Twain could not understand why anyone would waste a nice day hitting a small white ball, hunting it down, and then striking it again, over and over, until finally rolling it into a small cup, only to pluck the ball out of the hole and repeat the process seventeen more times.

However, one reason golf is so popular is that it *is* a "good walk." Players spend several hours in a beautiful natural setting often with emerald fairways, tall stands of stately old trees, azalea bushes bursting with new blossoms in spring, technicolor trees in fall, and the occasional white-tailed deer munching grass.

Mark Twain once wondered why anyone would waste a nice day playing golf.

Another reason to love golf (a reason Twain overlooked) is that it is good exercise; an 18-hole course forces a golfer to walk an average of five miles. The benefits of this physical exertion were noted by the *Times* of London, England, as early as October 5, 1874, when the newspaper commented: "There is exhilaration in the brisk walk round the links in the fresh sea air."[19]

But the greatest lure golf holds for those who fall under its spell may be that, for many players, it provides an outlet for the stresses of daily life. Al Geiberger, who in the 1977 Memphis Classic became the first to shoot a round under 60 (a 59) in a professional tournament, believes this aspect of the game makes it enjoyable for even the struggling player. "If you hit a bad shot," Geiberger says, "just tell yourself it is great to be alive, relaxing and walking around on a beautiful golf course."[20]

A beautiful tree-lined fairway at the Interlachen Country Club in Edina, Minnesota.

The Golf Course

The average 18-hole golf course is from sixty-five hundred to seven thousand yards long and has a par, the score a good player is expected to make on a particular hole, of 72 based on the sum of its holes, which are rated par-3, par-4, or par-5. The Rules of Golf, which govern the sport worldwide and are issued jointly by the United States Golf Association (USGA) and the Royal and Ancient Golf Club of St. Andrews (the R&A), define par as "the score that an expert golfer would be expected to make for a given hole."[21]

The rules stipulate a par-3 can be up to 210 yards long for women and 250 yards for men, a par-4 from 211 to 400 yards for women and 251 to 470 yards for men, and a par-5 from 401 to 575 yards for women and at least 471 yards for men. A few courses even have par-6 holes, which must be more than 575 yards.

Each hole consists of a tee area, in which players put their ball onto a wooden peg to hit their first shot; a fairway of short grass that is the intended route to the green; and the green, the smooth putting surface surrounding the hole. Bordering the fairway is rough, taller grass designed to penalize golfers for not hitting a straight first shot onto the fairway; it is much harder to hit a straight, long shot out of the rough. There is also very short grass called fringe, which encircles the putting area and rewards golfers who land their balls just off the green by making their next shot easier.

Golf course architects can create any type of hole imaginable—famed designer Pete Dye, for example, has popularized island greens and is noted for building deep-faced sand traps with steep sides supported by railroad ties. These devilish designers can make holes more difficult by incorporating hazards and obstacles such as trees, grassy mounds, ravines, lakes, ponds, streams, and even strategically placed rocks or boulders. Although courses may have the same par rating (72) and length (7,204 yards), no two are ever exactly alike. Bernard Darwin, grandson of naturalist Charles Darwin and one of the early twentieth century's finest golf writers, believes this variety separates golf from sports like football or soccer, whose athletic fields all have the same dimensions: "Golf differs

The island green, like this one in Myrtle Beach, South Carolina, is one of the golf course features that designer Pete Dye made popular.

from almost every other game in that every piece of land on which it is played has its own characteristics and scenery and flavor. It is no flat, bare expanse, but is made up of streams, hills and valleys, each with a personality of its own."[22]

A golf course, is essentially, an obstacle course. And to maneuver successfully through each shot, golfers must utilize the many different types of clubs they carry in their bag.

Golf Equipment

Winston Churchill, the prime minister who guided Great Britain through World War II, once joked that, "Golf is a game whose aim is to hit a very small ball into an even smaller hole, with weapons singularly ill-designed for the purpose."[23] Churchill's comment may have come after he suffered through a bad round, but its spirit captures the love-hate relationship golfers have with their equipment.

Many players who hit bad shots tend to blame their clubs, not their own faulty swings. Golfers are notorious for trying to improve by buying new, supposedly better clubs instead of working to eliminate the mistakes they make when they swing, (the real reason they shoot higher scores than they would like). To those who blame their clubs, Sam Snead, one of the greatest pro golfers ever, said "A workman is no better than his tools, [but] it is a poor golfer who blames his [clubs for poor play]."[24]

The most basic piece of equipment is the ball. There are many different brands but they are all the same size, weighing no more than 1.62 ounces and measuring not less than 1.68 inches in diameter, standards the USGA has enforced since January 1, 1932. The R&A for several decades preferred a slightly smaller ball before eventually agreeing to adhere to the American standard.

Golfers use a variety of clubs to maneuver their ball around a course, from a driver that can smash it hundreds of yards to a putter that may only tap it a few inches. There are two main types—woods and irons—but the name "woods" is inaccurate in the twenty-first century. Although the heads of these clubs once came from persimmon and other trees, today almost all are manufactured from metal. The newer clubs are sometimes called "metal woods," but because they have only been produced since the late 1970s most golfers still refer to them with the generic term "woods."

The woods are long-distance clubs and the 1-wood, also called the driver, is customary for the first shot on par-4 and par-5 holes. Woods are numbered from 1 to 9 and the most popular besides the driver are the 3-wood and 5-wood. Players sometimes hit tee shots with higher-numbered woods, either for greater accuracy on longer holes or to reach the green on longer par-3s, but they are usually used for second shots.

The hitting surface of the wood, called the face, is flat and has a great deal of rounded mass behind it. The higher the wood's number, the greater is its face angle, also known as loft. The greater loft combines with shorter shafts in the higher-numbered woods to produce increasingly higher, shorter shots. The driver has a loft of between six and twelve degrees, a preference left up to individual golfers, while face angles progress all the way up to thirty-four degrees for a 9-wood. Shaft lengths descend

from forty-three inches for the driver to thirty-nine inches for the 9-wood.

Irons are also numbered from 1 to 9 and have grooves, lines etched into the club face that impart spin to the ball so it will fly straight. The iron's slim, bladelike design enables golfers to strike the ball squarely even when it is nestled in tall grass or sand. Iron lofts range from seventeen degrees for the 1-iron to forty-eight degrees for the

GOLF COURSE ETIQUETTE

Golf etiquette is the term for the way golfers are supposed to act while playing. The following etiquette instructions are from *The Spirit of the Game,* a United States Golf Association pamphlet which leads off with this message from Arnold Palmer:

From the time I first stepped on a golf course, my father made sure that I observed golf etiquette. What that meant to me then, and what it means now, is being considerate of other golfers, taking care of the course, playing quickly, and controlling my temper. This code of conduct is a big part of what makes golf the greatest game of all. True golfers help protect the game by observing golf etiquette.

The pamphlet says that to practice proper etiquette, golfers should:

Always be aware of your safety and the safety of others. Safety—wait until the group ahead is out of range of your best shot. Safety—be sure you are well away from [your playing partners] before taking practice swings.

Stay silent and still while others in your group are teeing off [or putting].

Be ready to play when it is your turn to play, particularly on the putting green.

Smooth footprints and irregularities in sand after playing from bunkers.

Know how to repair a ball-mark [on the green]. Insert a repair tool or tee at the edges of the ball mark and bring the edges to the center. Do not lift the center of the ball mark. Try not to tear the grass. Repair your ball mark and others on the putting green. A repaired ball mark will heal in two to three days, an unrepaired ball mark will take three weeks to heal.

Mark your golf ball with a small coin or similar object. Stay off the line of putt of other players.

Treat others with respect. Treat other players the way you would like to be treated.

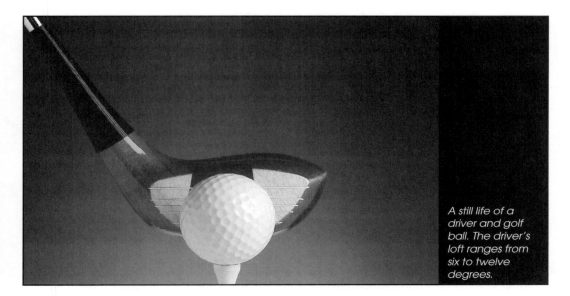

A still life of a driver and golf ball. The driver's loft ranges from six to twelve degrees.

9-iron, with greater lofts creating shots with increasingly higher, shorter trajectories.

Wedges are specialty irons that have more loft than 9-irons, as much as sixty-four degrees, and are used when the ball is close to the green or has landed in a sand trap. The most common are the pitching wedge and the sand wedge, clubs golfers use to hit high, soft shots that can land next to the hole. One of the easiest ways golfers can lower their scores is to become proficient with wedges.

Shaft lengths range from 39.5 inches for the 1-iron to 35.5 inches for the 9-iron and wedges. The putter, which can have a wide variety of shaft lengths depending on its style, is used to stroke the ball on the putting surface or from just off the green. Woods and irons made for women are generally an inch shorter overall than those for men.

In *The Complete Book of Golf,* John Allan May notes that most golfers do not carry every iron:

A regular set will comprise nine clubs: the 3- to 9-irons, pitching wedge, and sand wedge. There are . . . number 1- and 2-irons but they are more difficult to use. The 2-, 3-, and 4-irons are known as "long irons" and are used when good distance is required along with a higher flight. As the iron numbers get higher, a consistent player will hit the ball about 10 yards shorter with each club. The 5, 6 and 7 are "medium" irons and are used for middle distance shots. At close range—from about 130 yards in to the green—the "short irons" are used, the 8- and 9-irons, and the wedge.[25]

GENE SARAZEN INVENTS THE WEDGE

In 1932, Gene Sarazen invented the sand wedge. When he used it that same year to win the British Open, he showed the world of golf that his new club was one of the best weapons golfers could have to improve their play. *In the Wit and Wisdom of Golf: Insightful Truths and Bad Lies,* authors Al Barkow, David Barrett, and Ken Janke explain how Sarazen created the first wedge:

> The golfers of Sarazen's era, even the best of them, were generally poor players from [sand-filled] bunkers because they had to use a niblick [9-iron] with a sharp leading edge that dug too deeply in the sand. To mitigate the problem, Sarazen in 1932 conceived the idea of building a flange on the back of a niblick that was angled so the rear portion of it hit the sand before the leading edge. One could now hit behind the

ball without fear of digging too deeply. The ball would be exploded out on the force of the flying sand. After weeks of experimentation with his new club, Sarazen realized he had something special. "It got so I would bet even money I could [get the ball in the hole] in two out of the sand," he once recalled. That year he took his wedge with him to the British Open. During practice rounds he amazed everyone with his ability to play from the bunkers, and many people wondered about the "new weapon" in his bag. "After every practice round I put the club under my coat and took it back to the hotel with me," Sarazen recounted, "because if the British had seen it before the tournament began, they would have barred it. Once the tournament was underway, they couldn't do that. I went down in two from most of the bunkers [and won]."

Gene Sarazen blasts his ball out of a sand trap using his famous sand wedge.

Golfers do not use all the woods, either. The USGA in 1938 passed a rule limiting players to fourteen clubs, so each golfer has to decide which to carry. This choice is usually easy because individuals prefer the clubs they hit the best with; some players, for example, have more success with woods than irons or like to use several wedges with varying lofts. Thus, every golfer's bag will contain a different selection of clubs.

Golf Course Management

The real opponent in golf is the course, not another player. Clubs are the weapons used in the battle to defeat the course, but in order to shoot as low a score as possible, which is the object of the game, golfers must exercise good judgment prior to striking every shot. They must know which club to pull out of their bag, where to hit their ball, and how to best execute the particular shot. Golf is mentally demanding and players must constantly juggle a large number of variables and consider the consequences of every shot.

Collectively this mental process is known as course management, something that former pro star Johnny Miller believes is vital to playing well. "It's essential," Miller says, "to know where you want the ball to land. You must have a target clearly established in your head for every shot you hit, and that includes tee shots."[26] In 1974 Miller won eight tournaments and for several years was considered the best in the world. He believes even the worst golfer can shoot lower scores by mapping out a sound strategy for every hole:

> I know that the great players have always been great planners and that a sound game plan is essential in golf. To play good golf, you have to be prepared and pre-program yourself. I'll review each hole in my mind, pick targets for each shot, and go over the type of shots I will hit. It's like plotting a route on a map. You know where you're going, but unless you know the route and exit numbers before you start, you're liable to take a few scenic but unwanted detours.[27]

Before every swing, golfers should consider how best to avoid the rough and hazards that lie ahead of them, how to position their ball for the next shot, and factors such as the weather, the way the hole is configured (it may bend to the right or left), and their own strengths and weaknesses in hitting certain shots. Poor planning, as well as poor swings, can result in the "unwanted detours" Miller mentions, which can include disastrous journeys into trees, ponds, or sand traps.

Kinds of Shots

The tee shot is perhaps the most important on every hole. A long, straight drive will help a golfer reach his goal of par while an errant shot that lands in the rough or trees that border the fairway translates into trouble. Golfers strive for both accuracy and distance in drives, but it is wiser to place the ball in the fairway than to hit a longer shot into the rough. Because many golfers are more accurate with irons than woods, they sometimes hit irons off the tee, feeling it smarter to sacrifice distance for the sake of accuracy.

After a good tee shot, the golfer can hit directly toward the green. But if the ball winds up in trees, a sand trap, or other hazards, the golfer has to make a choice: go for the green or play a safe shot, which might even mean hitting the ball backward to return to the fairway. It is always best to take the safest route, even if it means sacrificing distance; harder shots tried from the trees or rough can often go astray, resulting in worse situations and additional strokes.

When the ball is close to the green, golfers use higher-numbered irons or wedges, not just to get the ball on the putting surface but to place it as close as possible to the hole so they have a chance to sink the ball with just one putt. When hitting to the green, golfers must take into consideration the putting surface's contours and

A tee shot gone astray. Many people ducked when this shot came their way, but the arrows show how the ball ricocheted off the head of one unfortunate fan.

the direction it slopes so they can calculate where the ball will roll after landing.

Once the ball is on the green, the player must figure out on what line to putt the ball so it will roll into the hole. This is not as easy as it sounds. Golfers have to mentally calculate a number of variables: how undulations in the green will affect the ball's path, how upward or downward slopes will influence the ball's speed, and how hard they must stroke the ball to keep it on the proper line. It is a complex mental process, one that must be mastered by every player.

The Golf Swing

The ability golfers have to maneuver around a course is dictated by their individual skill. But learning how to swing golf clubs properly and hit all of the required shots, from a long, powerful drive to a graceful, rolling putt, is difficult and takes a long time. There are many fine instructional books available that can help people learn to play. The very first was written in 1687 by Thomas Kincaid, a Scotsman who lived in Edinburgh. Following is one of his major principles: "In the swing you should maintain the same posture of the body throughout. Turn the body as far to the left in the downswing as you have turned it to the right in the backswing. AND the ball must be straight before your breast, a little towards the left foot."[28]

Kincaid's advice is as true today as it was more than three centuries ago. Although this

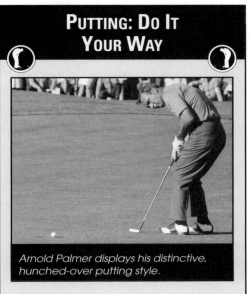

PUTTING: DO IT YOUR WAY

Arnold Palmer displays his distinctive, hunched-over putting style.

Putting is the part of the game that best allows people to express their individuality as players. There are many different types of putters and a wide variety of techniques to stroke the ball into the hole, and it is entirely up to individual golfers to choose the putter and style that best suits their personality.

In *The Story of American Golf: Its Champions and Its Championships,* Herbert Warren Wind explains that one of the most unusual techniques ever seen in the game's long history was tried in the 1895 U.S. Men's Amateur Championship:

In the main they were gentlemen-golfers (who were more gentleman than golfer), but among the entries there were a few characters, such as Richard Peters, who used a billiard cue on the greens, not because he wanted to clown around but because he was convinced he could putt better that way. [The pool-hall style was later outlawed.]

tip is simple and easy to understand, the swing is so complex that it would be impossible to explain it adequately in one chapter. The best way to learn to hit is to take lessons, something even professional golfers continue to do. "Don't be too proud to take lessons. I'm not,"[29] admits Jack Nicklaus, one of the greatest players in golf's long history.

There are two fundamental golf swing theories, however, that can help anyone who plays, especially someone just learning the game. Nancy Lopez, one of the best players ever, believes a smooth, controlled swing is the key to golfing well:

> My first rule is "distance without direction is worse than no distance at all." The key to having both distance and direction is making solid contact every time, and that's pretty hard to do if you are swinging out of your shoes trying to murder the ball. Most really good players swing at about 75 percent of full speed. That is a swing they can control but that will still deliver enough clubhead speed to hit a good drive. When they need a bigger drive, they increase their swing speed slightly, but never more than 90 percent, because anything faster than that is a swing headed out of control.[30]

The second bit of wisdom concerns the confidence golfers must nurture in themselves. In *Golf Is Not a Game of Perfect* sports psychologist Bob Rotella explains that golfers must never be upset by poor shots:

> One of the things Tom [Kite], or any successful pro, does best is to accept his bad shots, shrug them off, and concentrate completely on the next one. He has accepted the fact that, as he puts it, "Golf is not a game of perfect." [Kite] understands that while striving for perfection is essential, demanding perfection of himself on the golf course is deadly.[31]

Jack Nicklaus, one of the longest hitters in the history of golf, watches his tee shot during the 1983 U.S. Open.

Additionally, Rotella believes that golfers who learn to accept their mistakes instead of becoming angry will play better and have more fun: "When a shot is done, it's done. The only constructive thing you can do about it is to hit the next shot as well as you can. That requires that you stay optimistic and enthusiastic. Let the joy of the game come to you."[32]

A Good Game To Be Bad At

Forgetting bad shots is something golfers have to do every time they play. Although par for most 18-hole golf courses is 72, research by the National Golf Foundation in 1998 showed that only 22 percent of U.S. golfers regularly scored under 90 and the "average" player needed 100 or more shots to complete a round.

Despite these figures, millions of men and women continue to play a game they know they will fail at almost every time. They buy specialty equipment and take lessons in an attempt to better their scores. Whether they improve or not, however, is rarely an issue. They play simply because they love the game. A. A. Milne, the English author who created Winnie the Pooh, explains why even poor golfers can enjoy playing:

Arnold Palmer reacts with dismay after missing a putt during the 1970 Byron Nelson Classic.

Golf is so popular because it is the best game in the world in which to be bad. Sometimes I am tempted to go further and say that it is a better game for the bad player than for the good player. The joy of driving a ball straight after a week of slicing [is a delight] the good player will never know.[33]

CHAPTER 3

Evolving Through the Centuries

I<small>F A</small> S<small>COTTISH</small> golfer from the eighteenth century could be transported through time to St. Andrews today, he would be shocked by the changes that have taken place in nearly every aspect of this ancient game. Instead of the leather-skinned ball stuffed with feathers he once feared hitting too hard, lest it burst apart on impact, the old golfer would strike a hard-cased white ball that can fly almost three times as far. Instead of wielding a single wooden club, he would tote a bag loaded with irons and woods, some made of space-age metals not created until the twentieth century. To tee up his ball, the Scot would be handed a small, pointed piece of wood instead of the handful of wet sand he once used to form a small mound on which to place his ball.

The course would probably look familiar—the Swilken Burn, a small stream that has plagued golfers since 1754, still meanders through St. Andrews, and the gray, cold Atlantic Ocean still laps at the course's edges. But instead of shaggy, overgrown fairways where grazing sheep nibbled the turf, the ancient golfer would trod a well-manicured course and putt on greens with smooth, undulating grass surfaces shorter than any sheep could crop it.

He would remember the game the way British author Tobias Smollett described it in his 1771 novel *Humphrey Clinker:*

> In the field called the Links, the citizens of Edinburgh divert themselves at a game called Golf, in which they use a

curious kind of bat tipped with horn, and small elastic balls of leather, stuffed with feathers, [smaller] than tennis balls, but of a much harder consistence. These they strike with such force and dexterity from one hole to another that they will fly to an incredible distance. Of this diversion the Scots are so fond, that, when the weather will permit, you may see a multitude of all ranks, from the senator of justice to the lowest tradesman, mingled together in their shirts, and following the balls with the utmost eagerness.[34]

To this mythical Scotsman, twenty-first-century golf would look very strange. But he would quickly grow to love the many new refinements for one simple reason: they have all made golf easier to play and more enjoyable.

Golf Balls

The editors of *Golf Magazine's Encyclopedia of Golf* claim that over the centuries, the evolution of equipment has driven the most significant changes in the game. And the most significant changes have been due to new ball technologies:

Throughout history, golfers have crossed the Swilken Bridge (which spans the Swilken Burn) while playing at St. Andrews.

The history of golf is closely integrated with the history of its equipment. Actually, the history of golf, as we know it, could be divided into three periods, based on the type of ball used. The standard missiles during the early times [the twelfth century on] were the wooden ball and the leather-covered ball stuffed with either wool or feathers. The "feather-ball period" came to an end about 1848 with the introduction of the gutta-percha ball. Gutta-percha is a resin or gum from certain types of Malaysian trees of the sapodilla family. The "gutta-percha ball period" lasted until the turn of the century [1900], when we entered the "rubber-ball period" or the present era of golf.[35]

The primitive ancestors of today's high-tech balls were carved from wood, but during the 1500s the first major innovation led to the "feathery." These leather-covered balls stuffed with goose or chicken feathers only flew about 150 yards and when struck too hard could burst, scattering feathers everywhere. The delicate featheries rarely lasted more than one round and were expensive because a ball maker could only produce three or four per day.

The feathery was doomed by the advent of the gutta-percha ball, made from

MAKING A FEATHERY

It seems absurd today to think that golfers once played with balls stuffed with feathers. But the *feathery* was not a joke to golfers in that era or the artisans who labored several hours to make just one of them. In his 1890 book *Reminiscences by an Old Hand,* H. Thomas Peter explains the tedious process of making one of these quaint balls:

The making of first-class feather balls was almost a science. The leather was of untanned bull's hide. Two round pieces for the ends, and a stripe for the middle were cut to suit the weight wanted. These were properly shaped, after being sufficiently softened, and firmly sewed together—a small hole being of course left, through which the feathers might be afterwards inserted.

But, before stuffing, it was through this little hole that the leather itself had to be turned outside in, so that the seams should be inside—an operation not without difficulty. The skin was then placed in a cup-shaped stand (the worker having the feathers in an apron in front of him), and the actual stuffing done with a crutch-handled steel rod, which the maker placed under his arm. And very hard work, I may add, it was. Thereafter the aperture [hole] was closed, and firmly sewed up, and this outside seam was the only one visible.

Peter also notes that while the ball was being made, its feathers and covering were kept wet. When they dried the feathers expanded and the casing shrank, producing a sphere hard enough to play with.

Malaysian tree sap that is similar to rubber but hardens when exposed to the air. The Rev. Dr. Robert Adams Paterson, a professor at St. Andrews University who was also an avid golfer, is believed to have made the first gutta-percha ball in 1845. He molded it out of packing material wrapped protectively around a marble statue of the Hindu god Vishna that had been delivered to the school. Golf historian James A. Frank explains why the gutty (or guttie), as it was nicknamed, was superior:

> Golf made a quantum leap with the gutta-percha ball. The "gutty" was a bargain. The balls were cheaply and easily made by cutting chunks of the semi-hardened sap, then rounding them by hand or mold. The gutty lasted longer, flew farther, and rolled truer than the feathery, and if damaged, needed only a whack with a hammer or a run through a ball press to put it right.[36]

Long hitters could average 190 yards with their tee shots and drives of more than 300 yards with the new ball were recorded. The gutty's low cost and efficient design rejuvenated the game and helped spur golf's tremendous growth during the rest of the century.

The gutty era, however, lasted only until the end of the nineteenth century. During a visit in 1898 to a Goodrich Rubber Com-

pany plant in Cleveland, Ohio, Coburn Haskell, another golfing enthusiast, was inspired to invent a revolutionary new ball. Historian Herbert Warren Wind describes this turning point in ball technology:

> Haskell's attention was caught by a pile of thin rubber stripping, and he was struck by the idea that an improved ball might be built by wrapping these strippings tightly around a rubber core and covering them with a sheath of gutta-percha. With the assistance of a friend at the Goodrich Company, Haskell worked out the new rubber-cored ball, which revolutionized the game as thoroughly at the turn of the century as the guttie had done fifty years earlier.[37]

The new balls, also called "Bounding Billies" because of the way they bounced over the course when struck, flew twenty-five yards further on average than gutties. In 1901 British player John H. Taylor used the Haskell ball to win his second consecutive U.S. Amateur championship, and the following year Alexander Herd captured the British Open with them. The two victories helped assure the ball's acceptance by golfers.

However, not every innovation has worked. A few years later Goodrich manufactured a pneumatic ball featuring a pocket of air injected into its middle. Although this new ball flew a long way, it had a disturbing

WHY DO GOLF BALLS HAVE DIMPLES?

The surface of a golf ball is covered with nearly four hundred tiny concave depressions called dimples. In *Why Do They Call It a Birdie?,* author Frank Coffey explains why they are there:

> Why do golf balls have dimples (typically 382 or 384)? It's physics, the same aerodynamic principle used in the design of airplane wings. The dimples provide lift. When the ball is hit, it spins. As the ball comes off the club,

Even in this picture from the early 20th century, the ball the golfer is preparing to putt has dimples.

the dimples trap air in such a way that the air moves more rapidly over the top of the ball than the bottom, causing the ball to lift.

Dimples, however, began appearing on golf balls decades before those aerodynamic principles were even discovered. In *The History of Golf,* John Pinner explains that golfers first began to realize their value while playing with gutta-percha balls:

> The [gutty] was not an instant success. Much too smooth, it had a tendency to duck in flight. It was often remarked that the gutty flew better at the end of the round that it did at the beginning. It did not take long for someone to realize its performance improved after it had been cut about a bit by [clubs]. An experiment was carried out in which a newly molded ball was scored all over with the sharp end of a saddler's hammer. It proved highly successful, and the demise of the feather ball was inevitable.
>
> At first the markings on the ball were raised in what was called a bramble pattern. The concave marking known as the dimple was not patented until 1905, but within a decade it became standard for all balls.

tendency to explode in midflight or, even worse, while resting in the golfer's pocket.

Better Clubs, Too

The earliest players used just one club. But by the 1500s golfers were swinging several different kinds and by the early 1890s had so many they quit holding them in their hands between shots and started carrying them in bags. The first club shafts were made from ash or hazel, woods with a whiplike flexibility similar to bows; bow makers were the first craftsmen to manufacture golf clubs.

The heads were also wooden, but longer and narrower than woods are today. Club makers sometimes filled the heads with lead for extra weight or balance. When the gutty came into use, manufacturers began inserting pieces of leather, horn, or bone into the face to prevent damage from the harder new ball. They also began to wrap a soft material, usually sheepskin, around the top of the shaft where players gripped the club to ease the shock of hitting the harder ball.

The first irons were specialty clubs like the rutter, so named because its narrow iron head could scoop the ball out of wheel ruts, a common hazard. The names of these primitive irons have died out and sound strange today: a 2-iron was a "cleek," a 5-iron a "mashie," a 9-iron a "niblick." Fairway woods were generically referred to as "spoons," although a 2-wood was termed a "brassie" because of a protective brass plate

on its bottom. This nomenclature faded away in the 1920s when companies began producing full sets of clubs and numbering both irons and woods.

The introduction of the harder gutty increased the use of irons, which during the feathery period were impractical except for short, softly hit shots because their slim edge could injure the ball. Historian James A. Frank explains the changes the gutty caused in club design:

> To accommodate the harder ball, wood heads [formerly long and narrow] became shorter and squatter and were fitted with inserts, usually leather, for the first time. This era also saw hickory [a stiffer wood] become the choice in golf shafts. But, most significantly, irons came into their own. Unlike the feathery, the gutty could withstand an iron's blows (and, if not, the ball could always be remolded).[38]

Historian George Peper explains that just as the gutty changed the game, so did the Haskell:

> The softer wound ball needed a harder wood, and persimmon [with hard inserts] fit the bill followed by the laminated heads that would appear in the 1940s. Irons were made larger to give the livelier ball more time on the clubface, which improved [performance].

The quest for control also led to scoring iron faces with deep grooves meant to impart spin.[39]

Technological advances in ball making continued into the late twentieth century. The most dramatic came in 1968 when Top-Flite introduced the two-piece ball, which had a solid core of thermoplastic wrapped in a tough synthetic cover. The ball not only went further but its cover was harder to cut than the softer balata material previously used, which meant golfers did not have to buy so many new balls.

Bobby Jones, golf's greatest amateur player, strikes a shot with a 5-iron, a club known then as a mashie, at the Mid-Ocean Course in Bermuda in 1932.

Space-Age Technology

Frank Thomas, technical director for the United States Golf Association (USGA), ranks development of the Haskell ball as the twentieth century's number one advancement in golf technology. "The Haskell immediately lowered scores,"[40] he says. In addition, two other technological breakthroughs ranked second and third on Thomas's list: the steel shaft and perimeter weighting.

In the early 1920s golf equipment companies began making steel shafts, a huge advancement because a set of clubs could now have the same uniform strength and feel, which helps golfers hit more consistent shots. In the past, players had to sort through scores of clubs to find a set whose wooden shafts all had the same ball-striking qualities. The USGA approved steel shafts in 1925, St. Andrews six years later, and within a decade steel replaced hickory as the shaft of choice.

The switch to steel was such a huge leap forward that Thomas said "it brought shaft technology to a standstill for thirty years."[41] In the 1950s one company began using fiberglass, an innovation that failed, but in 1973 graphite was introduced and ignited a technological revolution that has continued into the twenty-first century. Graphite fibers bound together by resin created a shaft one to two ounces lighter than steel, enabling golfers to swing faster and hit longer shots; the greater the clubhead speed is when it strikes the ball, the farther the ball travels.

The success of graphite shafts led manufacturers to experiment with other material. Metal woods had first appeared in the 1890s, but they did not become popular until Gary Adams, the golf club innovator who founded Taylor Made and is known as "the father of the metal wood," began producing them in the late 1970s. The use of new metals and designs allowed clubheads of both woods and irons to become bigger and lighter, helping even less-skilled golfers hit the ball further and more consistently.

In a 1999 issue of *Golf Magazine,* Scott Kramer wrote that the adaptation of exotic

Modern metal clubs (top) allow golfers to hit better shots than did the older wooden clubs (bottom).

new metals pushed club development even further:

The engineering capability to mold light, space-age metals into clubheads has been the biggest reason for club advancement. Titanium revolutionized the driver market [in the 1990s] because designers—many from the high-tech aerospace industry—figured out how to form this ultra-strong and lightweight metal into the functional shape of a supersized clubhead. The result was a club golfers of any skill level could hit farther on off-center hits. The effective hitting area grew in direct proportion to the size of the head.[42]

A second major innovation in design was perimeter weighting, an old concept that Karsten Solheim, founder of Karsten Manufacturing Company and creator of Ping clubs, resurrected in the 1960s, first with a putter and then with irons. An engineer who took up golf at the age of forty-two, Solheim was the first modern club maker to distribute weight around the outside of the head. Because this technique expanded the club's sweet spot, the optimal spot to strike the ball, golfers who failed to swing perfectly were still getting solid hits.

However, the new irons could not have been produced without a metal fabrication process called investment casting. Peper explains the importance of this process, in which molten metal is poured into molds:

> Investment casting was not a new idea, although it did receive a big boost in the 1950s as the aerospace industry began to produce precision-made parts of lightweight, strong metal. When innovators [like Solheim] began experimenting with the casting of golf clubs,

they were picking up on an idea promoted as far back as the late 1800s: If the clubhead's weight could be spread out, distributed away from the small "sweet spot" in the center, less-than-perfect contact would still produce acceptable shots. Moving the weight toward the edges created a cavity on the back side of the club, hence the names "cavity-back" or "perimeter-weighted" irons.[43]

Golf Course Architecture

Early courses were as primitive as the featheries golfers used to play them. Peper notes how informally the first courses were designed:

> In Scotland, where the game of golf evolved, natural forces and grazing sheep [who burrowed into hillsides] were the first golf architects, carving hazards from the sandy, links terrain. The early players had only to choose the fairest patches of turf on which to hole out and the most reasonable and interesting route of play between holes. In America, the early courses had to be laid out on land provided not by nature but on sites selected by players.[44]

Because most Americans had never seen one, some early U.S. courses were poorly designed and would look strange today. An example of the bizarre layouts inflicted on

KARSTEN SOLHEIM: GOLF CLUB INNOVATOR

When he died February 16, 2000, at the age of sixty-eight, millions of golfers around the world owed a debt of gratitude to Karsten Solheim, the daring innovator who brought perimeter weighting to golf clubs. His willingness to try new ideas ignited a technological explosion which led to better clubs that make it easier and more fun to play golf.

As a child Solheim moved with his family from Norway to Seattle, Washington. An aeronautical engineer and inventor, Solheim began playing golf at the age of forty-two. He set out to design a club that would help him hit better shots, but ended up changing the way all clubs are made. When Solheim died, *Golf Magazine* commented on his importance to club design:

Solheim developed the revolutionary Ping golf clubs.

If you play golf, your life has almost certainly been affected by Karsten Solheim, best known for inventing Ping clubs. In the 1960s and 1970s, Solheim pioneered new designs for golf clubs. Tinkering in his garage, he built a putter with the weight concentrated in the heel and toe and a thin face that made a distinctive "ping" sound when striking the ball. A few years later, he developed irons with the weight around the perimeter of the clubhead; today, perimeter-weighted irons are the game's best sellers. "He paved the way for all of us," said Ely Callaway of Callaway Clubs [another manufacturer]. "He designed the first clubs that varied from conventional design. He changed it all."

early American golfers was noted in the November 6, 1897, issue of *Harper's Weekly* magazine, which kindly left out the course's name:

A player who has done a round at the —club will have passed over a steeple-chase course, race-track, polofield, and pigeon-shooting grounds [obstacles due to other activities the country club offered]; he will have come triumphantly through a purgatorial stonewall jump [for horses], a sand bunker and, finally, a vast gravel pit or crater. Stone walls, plowed fields, quarries, fences, and chasms are among the excellent sporting requirements of the course.[45]

Many courses, however, were well designed. Most golf clubs employed Scottish professionals like Willie Dunn, who in 1891 laid out Shinnecock Hills Golf Club in Long Island, New York, or Americans with Scottish roots like Charles Blair Macdonald, who learned the game when he attended St. Andrews University. In 1895 Macdonald built the nation's first 18-hole course, the Chicago Golf Club.

American Style

American courses have always looked different from Scottish ones because the land available had different topographical features. In *Golf: The History of an Obsession,* David Stirk writes that only Great Britain follows the "tradition of true links courses, with no trees and no landscaping or artificial lakes. Courses like St. Andrews are basically flat, though with a great many rough, deep bunkers and a sand dune or two."[46] U.S. links, on the other hand, were usually carved out of heavily wooded areas with large stands of trees guarding fairways, hills and rolling terrain, streams or ponds of water, and a variety of sand traps and other hazards.

U.S. course architecture was sent in a new direction by the Oakmont Country Club, which opened in 1903 outside Pittsburgh, Pennsylvania. Cofounder William Fownes wanted Oakmont to be a stiff test of golfing prowess, saying that, "A poor played shot should be a shot irrevocably lost."[47] To enforce his theory that players should be penalized for failing to follow the intended route to the green, Fownes included twenty-one drainage ditches, sharply tilted greens, narrow fairways, and nearly 220 bunkers.

Oakmont's design philosophy, which is called "penal," heavily influenced U.S. course construction until Augusta (Georgia) National Golf Club opened in January 1933. Augusta, designed by golfing great Bobby Jones and Scot Dr. Alistair Mackenzie, had fewer hazards than the penal style course and featured wide, gently rolling

Bobby Jones hits a shot while testing the Augusta (Georgia) National Golf Club course, which he helped design and which was still under construction.

"DYE-ABOLICAL" GOLF COURSES

Whistling Straits, a Pete Dye course on Lake Michigan in Haven, Wisconsin, is the most authentic Scottish links course in the United States.

Pete Dye was the most influential golf course designer of the twentieth century's last three decades. He was also the most controversial. Some reviewers even labeled his inventive layouts "Dye-abolical" because they were so hard to play and broke with traditional architectural principles.

A fine golfer who played in three U.S. Amateur Championships, Dye began designing courses in 1955 with his wife, Alice, the first woman inducted into the American Society of Golf Course Architects. When Dye's Tournament Players Club at Sawgrass course opened in Ponte Vedra, Florida, in 1981 it popularized two new features: large grassy mounds that offered spectators a spot to view tournament action and the infamous par-3 17th, an island hole surrounded by water.

Yet Dye also created Whistling Straits, which opened in 1998 in Haven, Wisconsin, and is truer to a Scottish links course than any other built in America. Laid out along two miles of Lake Michigan shoreline, Whistling Straits in 1999 was named by *Golfweek* magazine as one of the one hundred best modern courses and in January 2000 was chosen to host the 2004 Professional Golfers Association Championship. Waves pounding on the Lake Michigan shore, gently rolling terrain, waist-high marshy grass bordering the fairways which serves as a hazard to errant shots, and even a flock of grazing sheep; they all create the feeling at Whistling Straits that the golfer is in Scotland instead of Wisconsin.

fairways. Historian Wind claims Augusta stated the case for a new style of design that was named "strategic":

> As the home of the Masters, it demonstrated forcibly and handsomely the superiority of strategic design to penal design. There were only about thirty bunkers on the eighteen holes, and no rough to speak of. Its challenge lay in the imaginative use made of its wonderful rolling terrain and the creeks that crossed its lower stretches. Like every great course, [it] could be set up so that, from the back tees [which make it longer] it was a formidable test for the leading professionals, and, from the regular tees, a layout which the average golfer could handle and enjoy.[48]

Following the economic boom the United States experienced after World War II, thousands of new courses were constructed. Powerful new machines capable of moving tons of soil and irrigation techniques enabling green fairways to survive in the desert freed designers to use their limitless imaginations. The result was that the United States became home to more varied golf facilities than any other nation.

Architects with fresh new ideas created unique layouts like Grayhawk Golf Course in Scottsdale, Arizona, whose emerald fairways are bordered by sand and cactus, and the Tournament Players Club (TPC) at Sawgrass in Ponte Vedra, Florida, whose famous 17th green popularized island holes. But not all of America's newer courses are nontraditional. Jack Nicklaus, for example, has become one of the most prolific course designers around and one of his finest is Muirfield Village in Dublin, Ohio, which opened in 1974. Muirfield harks back to the classic designs of courses built in the early twentieth century such as Pebble Beach in California, Pinehurst in North Carolina, Winged Foot in New York, and Medinah in Illinois.

What To Wear

In addition to equipment and courses, another noticeable change has been in golf attire. Golfers today may wear shorts, a light shirt, and a hat or visor to block the sun, but a century ago the style was much more formal. Most men in 1900 wore heavy tweed coats modeled after British hunting jackets; they were usually red, a color adopted centuries earlier so nongolfers could easily recognize players in the common links they shared for recreational purposes. Men also wore ties, tweed caps, and "plus-fours," pants that were four inches longer than shorts. Although knickers were no longer fashionable after the 1930s, two-time U.S. Open champion Payne Stewart became famous for wearing them in the 1980s and 1990s.

Until recently, the formal clothes women wore were also so heavy and restrictive that

Ties, white shirts, cloth caps, and "plus-fours" were what the well-dressed golfer was wearing in the 1920s and 1930s. Today's golfers wear much more casual, comfortable clothing.

medals on the left breast in military style, deeply starched collars, a belt with broad webbing, and a huge buckle with club insignia or the owner's monograms, voluminous cloth or tweed skirts, and thick boots fastened with metal [studs]. On the golfer's head was usually a stiff boater [straw hat] with braids of club colors around the crowns.[49]

Better Golf

Advances in golf through the centuries have made the game more fun and helped players lower their scores. In 1767 James Durham recorded the first known score below 100 with a feathery when he shot 94 to win a tournament in Muirfield, Scotland. In 1858 Allan Robertson, playing a gutty, became the first to break 80 when he shot 79 at St. Andrews. In 1977 Al Geiberger, swinging with steel shafts, was the first to shoot a score under 60 in a professional tournament, a record 59 in the Memphis Classic, which he went on to win.

female golfers had trouble swinging. Golf historian Robert R. McCord describes a typical golfing outfit from the late 1890s:

A nineteenth century lady's outfit might have [included] red coats with buttons of gilt [gold] bearing the club crest,

CHAPTER 4

Golf's Greatest Champions

WHEN ALLAN ROBERTSON died in 1859, the *Dundee Advertiser* called the head greenskeeper of the Royal and Ancient Golf Club of St. Andrews (the R&A) "the greatest player that ever lived, of whom alone in the annals of the pastime it can be said that he was never beaten."[50] Yet the name of Robertson, the finest player of golf's feathery period, is not on any list of the game's great champions.

Although Robertson died before there were any major tournaments in which he could prove his skill, he was responsible for creating the British Open, the first tournament to gain worldwide stature. It was held the year after his death and its purpose was to determine his successor as the game's best player.

At that first British Open in 1860, eight golfers played three rounds over the 12-hole Prestwick Golf Club. Willie Park Sr. won by 2 strokes with a 174 total. Yet it was the man Park beat, "Old Tom" Morris, who became golf's first acknowledged champion.

"Old Tom" and "Young Tom" Morris

A native of St. Andrews, Scotland, Morris liked to say, "We were aw [all] born wi' webbed feet and a golf club in our hand here."[51] Morris was the first to win the British Open four times (1861, 1862, 1864, and 1867), a feat that made him legendary. Even a century after his death, photographs and caricatures of Morris are instantly recognizable; his tweed coat, plaid cap, full white beard, craggy features, and ever-present pipe are an enduring symbol of the game's Scottish heritage.

Morris captured his final Open at the age of forty-six years, ninety-nine days, and is still the event's oldest winner. The next year he was succeeded by his son, also named Tom, who won at the age of seventeen years, five months, a record even today for youngest champion in a major tournament. The Morrises were nicknamed "Old Tom" and "Young Tom" to tell them apart. Young Tom triumphed again the next two years and in 1872 won his fourth to match his father. Although Young Tom died only a few years later, Old Tom was a fixture at St. An-drews into the twentieth century as he su-pervised the course until 1904.

Francis Ouimet

In the early days of American golf, British and Scottish players like the Morrises regu-larly defeated their U.S. counterparts. But American golf finally came of age in 1913 when twenty-year-old Francis Ouimet stunned British greats Harry Vardon and Ted Ray with a win at the U.S. Open at the Country Club in Brookline, Massachusetts.

Ouimet was a polite, mild-mannered young man from a working class family. At eleven, he began working as a caddie at the Country Club. He obtained his first

"Young Tom" Morris shows off his British Open Championship belt (left) and is immortalized by an elaborate tombstone (right) at St. Andrews Cathedral cemetery in Fife, Scotland.

club by trading it for golf balls he found, and during his 1910 summer vacation worked in a store to earn $25 so he could join a local club. Just three years later, Ouimet was good enough to tie the two British stars after four rounds with a 304 total, forcing an 18-hole playoff for the Open title the next day.

Despite pouring rain, a huge, umbrella-wielding crowd trailed the players around the course. After nine holes, the trio were tied again at 38, but Ouimet made a 1-under-par birdie (one stroke below par) 3 on the 10th hole and a par-4 on the 12th hole for a 2-stroke advantage. Ouimet never surrendered the lead and finished at 72, 5 shots fewer than Vardon and 6 less than Ray. "I am as much surprised and pleased as anyone here," said Ouimet. "I simply tried my best to keep this cup from going to our friends across the water."[52]

In his 1933 book *A Game of Golf,* English journalist Bernard Darwin claims the playoff "was one of the most momentous of all rounds because, in a sense, it founded the American golfing Empire."[53] Ouimet's victory gave golf's popularity a tremendous boost: within a decade the number of American players exploded from fewer than 350,000 to more than 2 million.

Amateur versus Professional

One reason Ouimet was so warmly received was that he was an amateur. In 1913 golfers who played simply because they loved the game were more popular than professionals who made their living by giving lessons, designing courses, and managing golf clubs. In *The History of the PGA Tour,* Al Barkow writes that this prejudice grew out of Great Britain's rigid class system:

> American golf had as its heritage the British notion of social [and] economic place. The pros came from the working class and worked for the moneyed class, and the attitudes that prevailed between the two outside of golf carried into the game. However, as more and more American-born men became golf professionals, there was less and less of a feeling of subservience to the membership. The historical American egalitarian spirit began to prevail.[54]

Despite that attitude, people enjoyed watching pros play because they were so skillful. The first tournament with cash prizes was held January 1, 1898, at the Ocean Hunt and Country Club in Lakewood, New Jersey. Despite light snow in the morning and cold temperatures, ten pros played 36 holes for a total prize package of $150. After Val Fitzjohn and his brother, Ed, tied with rounds of 92 and 88, Val won a playoff to pocket the winner's share of $75. The *New York Times* noted the event drew "a large attendance, proving it a sporting event of greater interest than any that has been held here."[55]

FRANCIS OUIMET

When Francis Ouimet won the U.S. Open in 1913, he did more than prove an American could beat the best British players. An unassuming, modest young man from a working-class family, Ouimet shattered the era's negative perception that golf was a game only for the wealthy. In *The Story of American Golf*, Herbert Warren Wind claims that the way Ouimet changed public perceptions about the game helped golf grow tremendously in the United States:

> The luckiest thing that happened to American golf was that its first great hero was a person like Francis Ouimet. Had a pleasant young man from a good Fifth Avenue family or some stiff and staid professional defeated [Harry] Vardon and [Ted] Ray, it is really very doubtful if his victory would have been the same wholesale therapeutic for American golf that was Ouimet's. Here was a person all of America, not just golfing America, could understand—the boy from "the wrong side" of the street, the ex-caddie, the kid who worked during his summer vacations from high school—America's ideal of the American hero. Overnight the non-wealthy American lost his antagonism toward golf. He had been wrong, he felt, in tagging it a society sport. After

all, the Open champion was a fine, clean-cut American boy from the same walk of life as himself.

Francis Ouimet, the former caddie, became America's first great golf hero when he won the 1913 U.S. Open.

On April 10, 1916, in New York, the Professional Golfers Association of America (PGA) was created to promote professional golf. The association held the first PGA Championship that October at the Siwanoy Country Club in Bronxville, New York, with Jim Barnes defeating Jock Hutchison, and over the years it developed the PGA Tour, the annual schedule of pro tournaments in the United States.

Walter Hagen and Bobby Jones

The next two great golfers were a curious American pair—Walter Hagen, the first to make a living solely from playing, and Robert Tyre "Bobby" Jones, the game's greatest amateur. Although they both helped increase golf's popularity, their careers and personalities showcased the vast differences between professionals and amateurs.

In 1913 when Ouimet won the Open, Hagen was noticed not only for tying for fourth place but for his garish wardrobe: white flannel slacks, brightly striped shirts, and silk scarves, a sharp contrast to the drab tweeds worn by other players. Starting the next year with a U.S. Open victory, Hagen won five PGA titles, two U.S. Opens, and four British Opens.

This blacksmith's son once joked, "I don't want to be a millionaire, I just want to *live* like one."[56] Hagen did, spending money as fast as he earned it while becoming a cel-

ebrated star. The first golfer to support himself on tournament winnings, Hagen's flamboyant personality and great skill won him many fans and helped make pro golfers acceptable sports heroes.

On the other hand, money never mattered to Bobby Jones, who remained an amateur while winning thirteen major championships from 1923 through 1930 and is the only athlete honored with two ticker tape parades in New York City. His greatest achievement came in 1930 when Jones captured the British Amateur, British Open, U.S. Amateur, and U.S. Open, a feat nicknamed a "grand slam" after the *New York Sun*'s George Trevor wrote Jones had "stormed the impregnable quadrilateral of golf."[57]

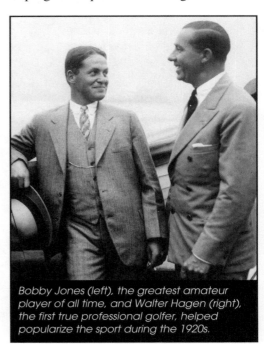

Bobby Jones (left), the greatest amateur player of all time, and Walter Hagen (right), the first true professional golfer, helped popularize the sport during the 1920s.

Citing what he called "the neurological nightmare of championship golf," the Atlanta, Georgia, native retired after 1930 at age twenty-eight. "There are two kinds of golf," Jones said, "and they are worlds apart. There is the game of golf and there is tournament golf."[58] Jones, however, remained devoted to the game, producing instructional films and books still considered classics. His crowning legacy was to found Augusta National Golf Club and the Masters Tournament, the first of which was held in Augusta in 1934.

Hogan, Nelson, and Snead

By a trick of fate, golfing greats have often appeared in threesomes. From the early 1890s into the 1920s three English players known as the "Great Triumvirate"—Vardon, J. H. Taylor, and James Braid—combined to win sixteen British Opens. During the mid-twentieth century, however, the United States received its own terrific trio in Ben Hogan, Byron Nelson, and Sam Snead, who all won major titles and helped make the fledgling PGA Tour a success.

Ben Hogan and Byron Nelson grew up together near Fort Worth, Texas. They both worked as caddies for local golf clubs and both excelled at the sport. Nelson was nicknamed "Lord Byron" and went on to set records in 1945 for the most PGA victories in one season (eighteen) and consecutively (eleven).

 THE PGA TOUR

In 2000 the Professional Golfers Association (PGA) Tour included more than thirty tournaments and total prize money of more than $150 million. This figure, however, belies the fact that the PGA Tour grew slowly during the twentieth century. In *The History of the PGA Tour*, Al Barkow explains how the first pro tournaments came about.

In 1917 *Golf Illustrated* magazine referred to the "grand tour" of Florida by pros during the winter. It might have been the first use of the word "tour" to describe a series of consecutive professional tournaments. In the spring the pros would work their way north through the Carolinas and Georgia before returning to their home courses in April, when they could start their jobs again [because winter was over].

PGA tournaments do not only enrich the golfers who compete in them. They also raise millions of dollars for charity, an aspect of pro golf Barkow said began early in the twentieth century:

The idea of turning over profits from a tournament to charity, after expenses, can be traced back to World War I. For instance, in June, 1917, a 72-hole professional tournament was played at the Whitemarsh Country Club in Philadelphia to raise funds for the Red Cross. This seems to have been the first played for this purpose.

Through the 1999 season, the PGA had raised over $500 million for U.S. charities.

Sam Snead (far left), Ben Hogan (second from left), and Byron Nelson (second from right) were three of America's best golfers.

Hogan, too, was a spectacular player. Nicknamed the "wee ice mon" by the Scots because he weighed only 140 pounds and played with an icy calm, Hogan captured nine majors and in 1953 came closer than anyone to a professional Grand Slam by winning the Masters and U.S. and British Opens. He is perhaps best remembered, however, for his remarkable comeback from a February 1949 auto accident that left him with a fractured pelvis and collarbone, broken ribs, and a broken ankle when his car collided with a bus.

Although many believed Hogan might never play again, he persevered through a painful rehabilitation. When Hogan left his Fort Worth, Texas, home for the 1950 Los Angeles Open, this proud golfer was not sure he would even play: "I'll just have to wait and see how I'm feeling and how my game is working. One thing I can tell you for sure: I'm not going out there and shoot in the eighties."[59]

Hogan tied Sam Snead through four rounds only to lose a playoff. But Hogan had proved he was back and later that year won his second U.S. Open, limping at times but playing brilliantly.

Although Hogan was noted for the precision of his swing, Snead's lacked grace.

"Snead doesn't know a thing about the golf swing," Hogan once joked. "But he does it better than anyone else."[60] Snead's free-swinging style accounted for victories in seven majors and a record eighty-one PGA tournaments.

Arnie and Jack

In 1954, after winning the U.S. Amateur Championship, Arnold Palmer turned pro and began making golf's popularity soar

Arnold Palmer peers over the shoulder of Jack Nicklaus at the 1973 Ryder Cup matches in St. Louis, Missouri.

like never before. Nicknamed "the King," he won seven majors and sixty-one PGA tournaments and his swashbuckling, daring style attracted hordes of fans known as "Arnie's Army."

Palmer's arrival corresponded with a regular schedule of televised golf. Although the British Broadcasting Corporation first telecast a match from London in 1938 and the sport's American debut was the final round of the 1947 U.S. Open, golf appeared only sporadically on television until the 1960s. PGA Tour historian Al Barkow claims Palmer's bold play made many new fans for the game:

> Television was beginning to be an important force in the game. The small screen in the tight frame is so intimate and revealing of character and personality, and Arnold Palmer, striding vigorously and obviously alive to every moment, could do nothing but light up the box and the game he played.[61]

Palmer's reign as "King," however, ended when he went up against an amateur from Ohio University named Jack Nicklaus. Although Palmer came from 7 strokes back on the final day of the 1960 U.S. Open to beat twenty-year-old collegiate star, in the next decade Nicklaus just got better and better. Nicklaus became so overpowering a golfer that when he won the 1965 Masters, Bobby Jones commented that, "He plays a game with which I am not familiar."[62]

The only professional to capture each of the four majors at least twice, Nicklaus, also called the "Golden Bear," won his sixth Masters in 1986 at age forty-six with a final-round score of 65. "I knew it was coming. I found the fellow I used to be out there,"[63] Nicklaus said after winning his record eighteenth major.

Tiger Woods

As Nicklaus aged, the golf world began to look for his successor.

Tiger Woods tees off in the third round of the 2000 Masters.

Called "Bear apparents" in a takeoff on the phrase "heir apparent," these would-be kings included Americans Tom Watson, Lee Trevino, and Johnny Miller as well as Spain's Severiano Ballesteros, England's Nick Faldo, Australia's Greg Norman, and South Africa's Nick Price.

They all dominated for a brief time, but it was not until Eldrick "Tiger" Woods turned pro in the fall of 1996 after winning a record three straight U.S. Amateur titles that a worthy successor truly emerged. Even Nicklaus admitted, "Some guys have come on and won a few tournaments, but nobody has sustained and dominated. I think we might have somebody now."[64]

Woods proved Nicklaus right by winning two of his first eight tournaments in 1996 and the Masters in 1997. In 1999 he set a tour record by earning more than $6.6 million and capturing the PGA Championship. And Woods was only twenty-three years old. Then, in 2000, he had perhaps the most amazing year in golf history when he won three of the four Majors—the U.S. Open, the British Open, and the PGA Championship—and set scoring records in all three tournaments.

Women Amateurs

With the exception of Bobby Jones, the most revered male golfers have always been professionals. Women, however, did not even have an opportunity to play professionally until the middle of the twentieth century. Before that, though, there were many great amateur players. One was England's Joyce Wethered, who in the 1920s won four British Ladies Championships and whom Jones once said was the finest golfer he had ever seen, man *or* woman. In a 1935 exhibition match on Jones's home course, East Lake in Atlanta, he beat Wethered by only three strokes, 71 to 74.

In the World War I period and the years immediately following it, the dominant U.S. woman was Alexa Stirling, a childhood friend of Jones. They both learned to play from East Lake professional Stewart Maiden, a Scot, and in 1908, when Stirling was twelve and Jones was six she beat him in a friendly match. "I have to be honest," Stirling admitted years later, "it wasn't very long until he was defeating me."[65] Starting in 1916, Stirling won three straight U.S. Amateur titles.

From 1922 to 1935, Glenna Collett, a long hitter who once banged a drive 307 yards, cap-

tured six U.S. Amateur championships and was hailed as "the female Bobby Jones."

The Babe

Sportswriter Paul Gallico once asked Mildred "Babe" Didrikson Zaharias if there were any game she had never played. "Yeah, dolls,"[66] joked the woman whom a 1999 Associated Press poll proclaimed the twentieth

Fans line the fairway in 1932 (top photo) to watch a match between amateur British and American women golfers. Joyce Wethered (bottom left) couldn't play professionally until the mid-twentieth century.

century's top female athlete. This multi-talented Beaumont, Texas, sports phenomenon won two gold medals (eighty-meter hurdles and javelin throw) and a silver (high jump) in the 1932 Olympics, was a basketball All-American in 1930 and 1931, and excelled in other sports including billiards, baseball, and figure skating.

Didrikson was born June 26, 1914, the sixth of seven children of Norwegian immigrants; her name originally ended in "-sen" but she changed the spelling to "-son." A tomboy who loved to play sports, she was nicknamed after George Herman "Babe" Ruth because of the home runs she hit while playing baseball.

Babe first played golf after the 1932 Olympics when challenged by sportswriter Grantland Rice. After hitting a thousand balls a day for several years to master the game, she won the Texas Women's Amateur title in 1935. For the next five years she played in the two or three tournaments open to women professionals and made money touring the country by performing in vaudeville and putting on sports exhibitions.

In 1940 Babe—her last name now Zaharias after marrying professional wrestler George Zaharias in 1938—was reinstated as an amateur. In 1946 she won the U.S. Amateur and in just two years captured seventeen important championships, including the 1947 British Ladies Amateur; she was the first American to win the prestigious title.

Although only five-feet-six-inches tall, Babe's long drives of 250 yards or more overwhelmed her opponents. While practicing in England, she was asked how she hit the ball so far. "I just loosen my girdle," Babe joked, "and let the ball have it."[67]

The LPGA

Babe used her popularity to help start the Ladies Professional Golf Association (LPGA), the first successful women's pro tour. In 1944 a group of top golfers formed the Women's Professional Golf Association, which two years later staged the first U.S. Women's Open won by Patty Berg. The group disbanded in early 1949, but that May thirteen players, including Babe Zaharias, a pro again after a company paid her one hundred thousand dollars to endorse its clubs, decided to form the LPGA.

The first LPGA event was the Tampa (Florida) Open, held in January 1950, and won by Polly Riley, a Fort Worth, Texas, amateur. The fledgling tour in its early years relied on well-known amateurs to draw fans and help fill out the sparse tournament fields. Louise Suggs was an early star and one of the LPGA's founders. In a January 2000 interview before the LPGA's fiftieth anniversary, Suggs admitted that starting the tour was a gamble: "I'm just glad I lived long enough to see this anniversary. We were a pretty gutsy bunch. We were so dumb we didn't know we couldn't succeed. I think we survived in spite of ourselves."[68]

AN OPPONENT EVEN BABE COULD NOT DEFEAT

Mildred "Babe" Zaharias was not only a great athlete, but a courageous one. Babe won five events in 1950 to lead the Ladies Professional Golf Association in earnings its first year with $14,800 and continued to dominate play until 1953, when she was diagnosed with colon cancer. But in *The Illustrated History of Women's Golf,* author Rhonda Glenn claims that even this dreaded disease could not sideline Zaharias for long:

> In one of the most inspiring victories in sports she won the [1954] U.S. Women's Open a year after a section of her colon had been removed because of cancer. The world cheered her remarkable recovery and the hopeful fantasized even cancer could not strike down this remarkable athlete.

However, the triumph was short-lived. Babe was back in the hospital in July 1955 and in December the dying golfer was released to spend her final Christmas with her husband and friends in Fort Worth, Texas. Glenn writes that Babe then made her final visit to a golf course:

> On December 26, Babe asked a friend to drive her to Fort Worth's Colonial Country Club. They pulled to a stop near the second green. "Babe got out of the car, in her bathrobe and pajamas," said Bertha Bowen. "She could

Mildred "Babe" Zaharias was one of the most popular female sports figures of all time.

barely walk. She just went over and knelt down and put her palm flat on the green. Then she got in the car and we went home." "I just wanted to see a golf course one more time," Babe said. Nine months later [September 27, 1956], she was dead.

Certainly, Babe was the LPGA's biggest drawing card and most dominant player, winning the U.S. Open in 1950 and again in 1954 in a dramatic comeback after a cancer operation. In *The Impossible Art of Golf,* editor Alec Morrison claims she was responsible for the tour's survival:

> With the same flair for showmanship as Walter Hagen (and much the same

ruthless competitiveness), Babe Zaharias was the real driving force behind
the founding of the LPGA. Perhaps
more than anyone, she determined the
standards of excellence which the
modern professional women's game
has achieved.[69]

In addition to Zaharias, there were many
other great players in those early years, including Suggs, who recorded fifty-five victories; Berg, a former U.S. amateur champion
who captured eighty-four tournaments;
Mickey Wright, who from 1958 to 1967 finished first eighty-two times and won a record
thirteen titles in a single year (1963); and
Kathy Whitworth, who holds the career
record with eighty-eight victories.

However, the LPGA did not flourish until
1978 when twenty-year-old Nancy Lopez
made a pro debut every bit as stunning as
that of Tiger Woods nearly two decades later.

Nancy Lopez

Lopez was a child prodigy who won the
New Mexico Women's Amateur when she
was twelve and tied for second in the U.S.
Women's Open in 1975 at eighteen. When
she joined the Pro Tour in 1978, Lopez
dominated the professionals right away,
winning nine tournaments as a rookie, including a record five in a row, and eight
more the next year.

Her intriguing background and sparkling
personality spread her fame far beyond the

Nancy Lopez smiles during her winning 1978 season.

world of golf. In *The Illustrated History of
Women's Golf*, Rhonda Glenn writes:

Nancy didn't arrive on the Tour, she
burst upon it. She won nine tournaments in 1978 and set a new money-
winning mark with $189,813. It is
difficult to comprehend the impact of a
single individual on an entire sport.
Miss Lopez had more pure charisma
than any player since the Babe, and the
game to go with it.[70]

Lopez helped increase the LPGA's popularity. The tour's annual prize money jumped
from $1.5 million in 1970 to $4.4 million in
1979, and in just a half century the LPGA
grew from only fourteen events with a total
prize money of $50,000 to forty-three events
in 1999 worth $36 million.

CHAPTER 5

The Changing Face of Golf

L EE ELDER STRUCK a golf shot on April 10, 1975, that sent a seismic shock through the once lily-white world of golf. That drive in the opening round of the Masters made him the first African American to walk the grounds of the Augusta (Georgia) National Golf Club as a player, not a caddie. After hitting a perfect drive, Elder strode down the first fairway in a tournament whose longtime chairman, Cliff Roberts, had once defiantly proclaimed, "As long as I'm alive, golfers will be white, and caddies will be black."[71]

As the twenty-fifth anniversary of his historic round approached in April 2000, Elder remembered his debut: "I didn't realize how important it was at the time, because all I really wanted so badly to do was play in the tournament. It didn't dawn on me what had happened until after I played. Before then, I don't think I knew what a big deal it was."[72]

Elder appeared in the Masters fourteen years after the Professional Golfers Association of America (PGA) rescinded its rule barring nonwhites; Article Three, Section One of its 1916 constitution had limited membership to Caucasian professionals. Although baseball had rejected its own racist past in 1947 when Jackie Robinson played for the Brooklyn Dodgers, it was not until 1961 that the PGA relented. Even though Elder failed to make the cut to play in the final two rounds of the 1975 tournament, his appearance was significant: Augusta National was no longer forbidden to African Americans.

As a result, golf's most significant social development during the twentieth century was the increased access African Americans and other minorities, juvenile golfers (those aged twelve to seventeen), women, and even athletes with physical disabilities won to play a game they loved.

A Pastime for the Rich?

Although golf at times has excluded some people from playing, its origins were democratic. In *The History of Golf*, John Pinner writes that the first seaside links were open to anyone: "In the early days of golf in Scotland, the game was played on rough common ground without any thought of class distinction, and the only class recognized was that of skill at the game."[73]

Tiger Woods embraces Lee Elder (left) after winning the Masters Championship in 1997.

As the sport became popular in Great Britain, golf developed into a game played mainly by members of royalty and people rich enough to join exclusive clubs. Even when the sport caught on in America, it was still mainly played by the upper classes. Historian Marcia Chambers writes,

> Golf began as one of the outdoor pastimes of the very rich. It did not get developed [in America] as a sport of the people, as did baseball, or, later, basketball [but] as part of the world of private leisures, first on the estates of the very wealthy and soon after at the private country club.[74]

The nation's first public course, Van Cortlandt Park, opened in 1895 in Riverdale, New York, but even at the beginning of the twentieth century most U.S. golf clubs were private. Also, the United States Golf Association (USGA) and other organizations that regulated golf were run by rich whites. The result was discrimination against African Americans, Jews, and other minorities.

KINGS AND PRESIDENTS

Although golf is enjoyed today by average people, for centuries it was a pastime chiefly for the wealthy and powerful. In *Presidential Lies: The Illustrated History of White House Golf,* Sheperd Campbell and Peter Landau note that Spain's King Juan Carlos, Monaco's Prince Rainier, and Bhutan's King Jigme Singye Wangchuck all played. But they claim the most "zealous royal golfer" was King Hassan II of Morocco: "Hassan had a nine-hole course built on his palace grounds. [A round] could begin at any hour, since the king had the whole layout lighted. Lee Trevino . . . said Hassan had 'servants walking right down the fairway carrying trays of water, soft drinks, and food.'"

American presidents have had a long love affair with golf, and in 1909, William Howard Taft became the nation's first golfing chief executive. Campbell and Landau say thirteen of the next sixteen presidents all played; only Herbert Hoover, Harry Truman, and Jimmy Carter were nongolfers. Woodrow Wilson was such an avid golfer that he played on April 2, 1917, just hours before asking Congress to declare war on Germany.

The most tragic presidential linksman was Franklin D. Roosevelt, who loved the game but was never able to play again after contracting polio in 1921. According to Campbell and Landau, Roosevelt's wife, Eleanor, once said, "Golf was the game that Franklin enjoyed above all others. After he was stricken with polio, the one word that he never said again was golf."

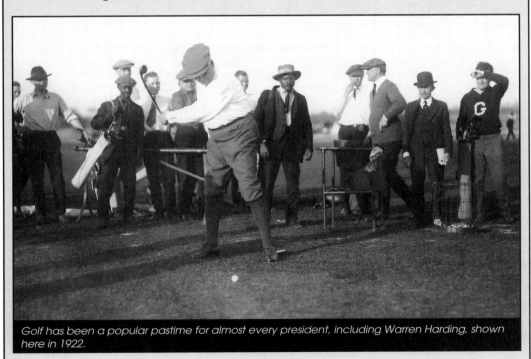

Golf has been a popular pastime for almost every president, including Warren Harding, shown here in 1922.

Caucasians Only

In 1896 racism made an ugly visit to the U.S. Open. Two of the entrants in the tournament at Shinnecock Hills were John Shippen, who had helped build the course and gave lessons there, and Oscar Bunn. When white professionals discovered Shippen's father was African American and his mother a Shinnecock Indian—the course is named after the Native American tribe that once ruled the area—and Bunn was also a Shinnecock, they refused to play.

United States Golf Association (USGA) president Theodore Havemeyer, however, firmly informed the other golfers that "we are going to play this thing today even if Shippen and Bunn are the only people in it."[75] The pros had no choice but to accept the minority golfers. Shippen shot 78 to tie for the first-round lead, but a second-day 81 dropped him into a tie for fifth. Still, he had made history as the first African American to play in a major tournament.

Generally, however, African Americans were excluded from the white world of golf. Country clubs welcomed them as caddies and cooks but barred them from playing, and even public courses turned them away. Yet the racism that forced them to travel one hundred miles or more to find a course to play could not keep them from enjoying the game. In 1921 a writer for the *Chicago Defender,* an influential African American newspaper, explained the sport's appeal:

> The reason for its popularity is that golf captivates from the instant one begins to play. In short, it is the universal game—the superlative in athletics—the most democratic, the most rational, the most exhilarating, beneficial and enjoyable pastime yet invented by man.[76]

Because white country clubs refused them membership, African Americans created their own facilities. The Shady Rest Golf and

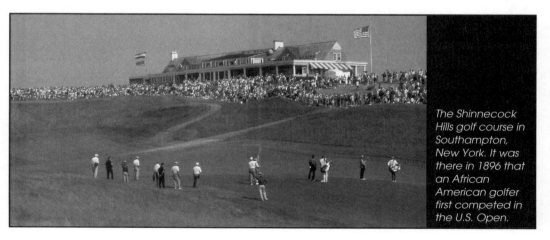

The Shinnecock Hills golf course in Southampton, New York. It was there in 1896 that an African American golfer first competed in the U.S. Open.

Country Club in New Jersey and the Citizens Golf Club in Washington, D.C., were two such places, both in operation by 1921.

United Golf Association

African American professionals had to go a step further than their amateur counterparts, who only sought a place to play a friendly round. In 1926 they created the United Golf Association (UGA), an organization similar to the Negro Leagues that began in the 1920s because of major league baseball's color barrier. UGA stars included Lee Elder, Charlie Sifford, Bill Spiller, Pete Brown, and Teddy Rhodes who won more than 150 UGA tournaments.

A 1960 letter written by golfer Bill Spiller (right) sparked debate over the 1916 law that banned minorities from playing in any of the country's most prestigious golf tournaments.

UGA events offered little prize money, and top players like Spiller and Rhodes, angry they could not enter the richer PGA tournaments, repeatedly tried to overturn the racial ban begun in 1916. It was not until 1961, however, that the PGA rescinded its racist policy, and it took a judicial threat to force that change. In 1960 a letter Spiller wrote outlining the injustice was sent to California attorney general Stanley Mosk, who realized the prejudicial policy was unconstitutional because it deprived African Americans of their civil rights.

Mosk informed the PGA it could no longer hold segregated tournaments in Cali-

fornia, including the 1961 PGA championship. The PGA tried to sidestep the issue by saying it would use only private facilities. But in *Forbidden Fairways: African Americans and the Game of Golf,* Calvin H. Sinnette, an African American doctor and golfer, explains that Mosk did not back down:

> Fearlessly, Mosk countered by telling the PGA it would not be allowed to circumvent his ruling by using private courses. Moreover, Mosk notified . . . other states of the action he had taken. Faced with the realization that Mosk was . . . resolute in his determination to implement the ruling, the PGA capitulated [gave in]. In 1961, the offensive and disgraceful "Caucasian Race"

clause was deleted. A shameful chapter in American golf history had finally come to an end.[77]

Several UGA stars made a successful transition to the PGA. Sifford in 1967 became the first African American to win a PGA tournament when he finished first in the Hartford (Connecticut) Open.

Minority Gains

When segregation laws were struck down in the 1960s, African Americans gained access to more courses. But even after Jim Crow laws were declared illegal, it was not always easy to enforce the new laws, especially if a golfer were a woman as well as an African American.

Ann Gregory was one such player who on September 17, 1957, teed off in the U.S. Women's Amateur to become the first African American woman in a national championship. Despite her sterling qualifications as a golfer, Gregory still faced discrimination while living in Gary, Indiana, during the 1960s. In fact, she, along with

Four African American women golfers pose for a picture in 1952. At that time there were few minority players and women golfers were rarer still.

other African Americans, was only allowed to play a 9-hole course at Gary's Gleason Park instead of the regular 18-hole layout reserved for whites.

But Gleason Park was a public course funded by local government, and one day Gregory decided she had had enough of discrimination. She paid the fee for the longer course and proclaimed, "My tax dollars are taking care of the big course and there's no way you can bar me from it. Just send the police out to get me."[78] She boldly walked to the first tee, played the entire course, and after that had no more problems.

The Tiger Effect

Despite increased access to courses and some early successes, African American interest in golf grew slowly during the 1970s and 1980s. It wasn't until Tiger Woods came along that things began to change. Woods was so incredibly popular that he single-handedly created an upsurge of interest in the game among African Americans, other minorities, and young people, thus altering golf's demographics.

The National Golf Foundation (NGF) reports that just three years after Woods turned pro in 1996, the African American golf population had increased to nearly nine hundred thousand, an astonishing 100 percent jump since 1991. The foundation also noted that the number of junior golfers, many of them African American, had risen 34 percent in the same period to 2.4 million.

The NGF attributed both jumps to Woods. After Tiger won his sixth straight tournament in February 2000, PGA Tour spokesman Bob Combs commented on the phenomenon: "He is bringing new fans to the game. We see more kids and minorities, all because of Tiger."[79]

The result of those changes was evident one day in late 1997 at Tilden Park, a municipal course in Berkeley, California. David Pillsbury, president of the firm that operates the course, was amazed by the scene:

I was looking around the practice greens, and it was one of the most profound things I'd ever seen. On one end was a bunch of teenagers, boys and girls, hanging around, putting and talking, having a good time. Not far from them, you had a guy with purple hair practicing his stroke. Everywhere you looked on that green, you saw something different. African-Americans, Asian-Americans, Hispanics, women, kids, blue-collar guys. You name it and they were out there.[80]

Other Minorities Play

By the end of the twentieth century, members of other minority groups that had traditionally ignored the sport were flocking to golf. In 1998 amateur Jenny Chuasiriporn tied professional Se Ri Pak of Korea after four rounds of the U.S. Women's Open at

Blackwolf Run in Kohler, Wisconsin. Chuasiriporn lost a playoff the next day, but it was a remarkable performance by the Duke University student, whose parents had immigrated from Thailand in 1970. Further, Woods's Stanford University teammates included Notah Begay, a Native American who in 1999 won his first two PGA tournaments, and Will Yanigasawa, a Chinese American.

One young player who is part of golf's increasingly multicultural future is Henry Liaw, a Chinese American from Rowland Heights, California, who in 1999 at the age of thirteen was considered one of the nation's top junior players. Known for his long 250-yard drives even though he is just five-foot-six, Liaw (whose name rhymes with "pow") was already being considered a potential professional star. Liaw, though, was taking his career one step at a time: "My main . . . reason why I want to play golf is to get a scholarship and go to college. Golf is a lifetime sport. You can play it a long time. I intend to do that."[81]

Showing just how much the game has evolved, a 1999 survey by the NGF indicated that nearly 10 percent of all U.S. golfers are members of a racial minority. That figure even in-cludes 851,000 Asian or Pacific Islanders and 712,000 Native Americans, Eskimos, and Aleuts.

Women Struggle, Too

Even though Mary, Queen of Scots, and others played golf from its earliest days, women have traditionally had trouble being accepted as equals in a sport controlled by men. Historically, they have had to fight for the right to play on many courses and to be taken seriously as competitive athletes. Historian Herbert Warren Wind claims that American men even actively tried to keep women off their courses:

Babe Zaharias (second from left) joined the ranks of athletes as famous as golfer Sam Snead (center) and Boston Red Sox hitter Ted Williams (far right).

The early golfers liked to find pretty women lounging on the verandahs of their clubhouses, but they were not in favor of women playing the game. To keep them off the course, the men invoked stringent club rules, argued the fantasy that golf developed unbecoming muscles, and talked loud about the dangers lurking on the wild frontier bordering the holes farthest away from the clubhouse.[82]

Despite those threats, stars like Mildred "Babe" Zaharias began to emerge during the twentieth century as more females began participating in a wide variety of sports. As a result, women—white women, that is—began to have an easier time gaining acceptance. But as late as the 1990s, many women were still denied equal rights at private country clubs, whose governing committees were dominated by men. In *The Unplayable Lie: The Untold Story of Women and Discrimination in American Golf,* Chambers contended that even as recently as 1995, country clubs still subjected women to forms of discrimination and prejudice unparalleled in almost any other part of their lives. She wrote,

At many country clubs they [women] cannot [become full members] even though their money may be paying for it. They have no right to vote in club affairs, no real say in the governance of

MARY, QUEEN OF SCOTS

Mary, Queen of Scots, made an important contribution to the sport of golf.

In *The Illustrated History of Women's Golf,* Rhonda Glenn writes that Mary, Queen of Scots, one of the first woman golfers, made a lasting contribution to golf:

Mary was an avid player. She took to the Scottish linksland with vigor, even making an appearance or two at St. Andrews. Her lasting contribution is the origination of the word *caddie,* which came about when Mary brought a number of *cadets,* sons of French noblemen who served as pages, back to Scotland [from France, where she grew up]. The Scots pronounced the French *cadet* as "caddie." Sporting a great pleated collar and heavy gowns of silk and rich velvet, Mary strolled with her *cadets* around Scotland's first golf links; so crude were the links that players agreed to a starting and ending point [for the course] to determine the length of a round.

club life. Desirable weekend tee times are often unavailable to them simply because they are women, even if they have paid the same membership fees as a man. And when they wish to top off a round of golf with lunch, they may find that the only place open is a men's grill, to which they are denied entry. Even at the public courses they may find that no matter how good their game, they are treated unfairly.[83]

Chambers also wrote that women who belong to country clubs are sometimes referred to as WORMS—Wives of Regular Members—because memberships are in their husbands' names. If those women become widowed or divorced, they often lose their country club privileges.

Despite such problems, more women than ever before were playing golf at the end of the twentieth century—5.7 million according to a 1998 NGF study. And although women in 1998 accounted for only 22 percent of all U.S. golfers, the NGF said their numbers had increased dramatically during the 1990s, rising by 24 percent, and that females accounted for 39 percent of all beginning golfers.

Handicapped Golfers

Although the sport is demanding even for people in top physical condition, thousands of golfers who have lost limbs, been blinded, suffered strokes that impaired their muscular control, or have other disabilities can still participate. In an article in *WE Magazine,* a publication on disabled lifestyles, Guido P. Cribari writes that increasing numbers of the disabled were playing at the end of the twentieth century:

Out on the course, where it counts, golfers with disabilities are making their presence felt in tournaments and during casual rounds. The 1990 passage of the Americans with Disabilities Act and the high-profile accessibility suit won against the PGA by pro golfer and *WE* contributing editor Casey Mar-

Disabled golfer Casey Martin won the right to use a golf cart, something other players cannot do, after he filed a lawsuit against the PGA Tour.

tin have driven the golf world, from rank amateurs to touring professionals, to reassess its previous misconceptions and downright ignorance of the significant numbers of golfers who play with disabilities. On any given day across the land, devoted duffers who are blind, mobility-impaired or recovering from recent hip or knee replacements play the front and back nines of the nation's golf courses all the while driving, chipping and putting the ball as equals.[84]

Casey Martin, for example, who suffers from Klippel-Trenaunay-Weber syndrome, a degenerative circulatory disorder that withered his right leg, has become the most famous disabled golfer in the game's history. When Martin attended Stanford University and was a teammate of Tiger Woods, he walked the course like everyone else despite his leg's lack of strength and the pain it caused. But by the time Martin wanted to play professionally on the Nike Tour, a minor league circuit, his leg had deteriorated and he needed to ride a motorized golf cart between shots. When the PGA refused to let Martin ride, claiming it would give him an unfair advantage over golfers who had to walk, he sued under the Americans with Disabilities Act. Ultimately, Martin prevailed.

Riding a cart in 1999, Martin won the Nike Tour's first event and finished fourteenth in overall earnings to qualify for the

BLIND GOLFER

When Bill McCafferty went blind in 1989 due to congenital vision problems that had plagued him all his life, he thought he would never be able to golf again. The Seaford, Delaware, player was wrong.

In 1992 a friend, David Gaynor, lured him back to the game. After learning to play again even though his sight was gone, McCafferty became a member of the United States Blind Golfers Association. On his Internet website—Golfing Blind Is Not a Handicap—McCafferty explains what it is like to play blind:

> Whereas, before I was able to walk the fairway independently, eye the ball, choose the right club, perfect my swing, drive the ball and watch to see where it landed, I now rely on a coach to be my eyes and tell me in which direction to aim the ball in relation to my position, what physical obstacles are part of a particular hole and where the ball has landed. Otherwise, it is the same sport. I still choose the club, perfect my swing, drive the ball, enjoy the game and the challenge to become as great a golfer as possible.

PGA Tour. In January 2000 Martin teed off in the Bob Hope Chrysler Classic near Palm Springs, California, to become the first golfer ever allowed to ride a cart in a PGA tournament. Martin was besieged by the media even though he did not do well. "Only a handful of players get this kind of attention," Martin noted. "Hopefully, someday I'll do something to deserve it."[85]

Improvements for Disabled Golfers

Martin's case is special—he is a golfer with a disability who is good enough to compete with professionals—but there are thousands of physically challenged athletes around the world who simply want to play recreationally. For example, in 1981 Greg Jones, who contracted polio when he was three years old, recorded a rare hole in one even though he has to swing while propping himself up with a crutch under his left arm. Jones, who lives in Denver, Colorado, and in 1992 founded the Asso-

ciation of Disabled American Golfers, says disabled golf has a long history:

> Disabled golfers, as a group, has been growing in recent years, but it kind of started after World War I in England, mostly with people that had an arm blown off [in the war] but still had their legs. They even have a one-armed golfer society over there, so it's been going on for a long time.[86]

Many disabled golfers like Jones have banded together to make it easier for them

Many disabled golfers enjoy the game despite physical problems.

to play a game they love. The United States Blind Golfers Association has aided blind and visually impaired golfers since 1953 and the National Amputee Golf Association and Physically Limited Golfers Association helps people with a variety of disabilities play. Jones said the 1990 Disabilities Act, which sought to end discrimination against people with handicaps, has had a tremendous impact in motivating and helping the disabled to play golf and other sports.

The United States Golf Association and the Royal and Ancient Golf Club of St. Andrews have even issued revised rules for the disabled that make it easier for them to play and compete with able-bodied golfers. One important change is that disabled players can ground their clubs in a sand trap. Normally players are not allowed to ground their clubs (touch the sand with them) be-fore hitting a shot out of a trap. But this is something disabled golfers must have to do to find the ball, if they are blind, or need to steady themselves before swinging.

Golf Opens Its Doors

As the twentieth century ended, golf was beginning to accept and embrace a wide variety of players. As a symbol of those social changes, Tiger Woods, whose ethnic heritage is a rich mixture of African American, Asian, Native American, and Caucasian, understands the importance of golf's transformation. He says, "Golf was originated in Scotland by rich whites. When it was brought over here, we made our country clubs exclusively for whites. Minorities, they just served as cooks, porters, and caddies. So it's refreshing to see some changes happening."[87]

Twenty-First-Century Golf

GOLF BEGAN IN the fifteenth century as an obscure athletic endeavor enjoyed by only a few men and women on the Scottish sea coast. By the dawn of the twenty-first century, the seventh in its long history, golf was a wildly popular game played around the globe. There are no definite answers to the question of why gold became so popular, although many people offer ideas.

Golf's popularity may lie in its ability to cast a spell on people of every race and all walks of life. According to Henry Long-hurst, an early–twentieth–century British writer, golf is "the 'Esperanto' or universal language of sport. Indeed, golf crosses cultural barriers and fits into various societies because it meets the needs of the people. There's something in golf for everybody."[88]

Through the centuries golf has, indeed, leapt across international and cultural barriers. Although several of the original thirteen rules set down in 1744 by The Honourable Company of Edinburgh Golfers are still observed, others have been dismissed, changed, or entirely altered to help the game adapt to new locales. For example, a rule once posted at the Nyanza Club in British East Africa said: "If a ball comes to rest in dangerous proximity to a hippopotamus or crocodile, another ball may be dropped at a safe distance, no nearer the hole, without penalty."[89] Needless to say, this is not a rule that appears on courses in New York, London, or Tokyo.

Sir W. G. Simpson, one of golf's earliest and most celebrated chroniclers, offered yet another suggestion for the game's mass appeal in his 1887 book *The Origin of Golf.* Simpson noted that unlike other sports whose players had to be fine athletes, almost anyone could play golf: "There is no shape nor size of body, no awkwardness nor ungainliness, which puts good golf beyond one's reach. There are good golfers with spectacles, with one eye, with one leg, even with one arm."[90]

Whatever the reason, the universal fascination with golf continues today in an era in which it has never been easier for people to learn the game.

High-Tech Golf

The great Ben Hogan once said "no one has ever conquered golf and no one ever will."[91] But in the new millennium, equipment manufacturers are trying harder than ever to help average players achieve that elusive goal.

This mountain climber, driving a ball off the edge of a towering peak, symbolizes the limitless possibilities that golf offers its participants.

After advancing in the previous century from hickory to steel to graphite, one company in 2000 was producing shafts from an alloy of aluminum and scandium, a rare metal used to build Russian fighter planes. Another firm made woods and irons from so-called "super steels." And a third boasted a new technique enabling it to create irons with "variable face thickness," a feature that allowed designers to optimize weight distribution for better shots. Several other companies continue to try to reinvent the ball.

The dramatic changes that have occurred in clubs and balls over the centuries have made golf easier, cheaper, and accessible to more players, a factor that has helped foster the game's continued growth. But the benefits golfers derive from modern technology are by no means limited to their equipment.

Golfers today use computers with modems to make a reservation to play, find the best price on a new driver, download a picture of a beautiful course, or track down a golf tip that will stop them from slicing the ball. In *Access* magazine, Sean Nolan writes that players are using the Internet to

> tune up their golf game with online tools that add a new dimension [to instruction]. Zeroing in on proper mechanics requires a clear understanding of minute details such as stance, club alignment and follow-through. The Web can break down those minute details into frame-by-frame clips that make instruction easy to absorb.[92]

Players today can also record their swings with video cameras to see what they are doing wrong, practice at automated driving ranges where their ball is mechanically placed on a tee, and leisurely navigate the course in a golf cart. They can also watch golf twenty-four hours a day on the Golf Channel, the cable channel that began in 1995 and is now seen in the homes of more than 20 million viewers.

Golf's Essence Is Intact

Despite such modern embellishments, golf is still basically a low-tech athletic pursuit, one in which success depends more on physical skill and emotional control than technological advances. A ball today may travel farther when it is struck, but that is of no help to the golfer who cannot hit it straight. Thus the essence of the game has remained unchanged since golfers wielding wooden-shafted clubs tried to knock a ball stuffed with goose feathers onto a grassy green trimmed by grazing sheep.

In his 1975 book *The Story of American Golf,* Herbert Warren Wind traced the evolution of this ancient sport from its birth in Scotland. Although he chronicled the myriad changes that had taken place in the game, many of which he witnessed firsthand as a journalist for more than a half century, Wind wrote: "Over the last hundred years, golf has changed in many ways but, essentially, golf has remained the same strange, elusive, maddening, beckoning, wonderful game it has always been."[93]

Despite the fact that the pace of golf's evolution became even faster in the last quarter of the twentieth century, Wind's words were just as true in 2000 as they were when he penned them. Golf is still a wonderfully maddening pursuit, one that can humble even the greatest players and whose fundamental nature no amount of high-tech equipment or other improvements will ever be able to alter.

Statistics

The Masters Champions
(Augusta National Golf Club)

Year	Winner	Score
2000	Vijay Singh	278
1999	Jose Maria Olazabal	280
1998	Mark O'Meara	279
1997	Tiger Woods	270
1996	Nick Faldo	276
1995	Ben Crenshaw	274
1994	Jose Maria Olazabal	279
1993	Bernhard Langer	277
1992	Fred Couples	275
1991	Ian Woosnam	277
1990	Nick Faldo	278
1989	Nick Faldo	283
1988	Sandy Lyle	281
1987	Larry Mize	285
1986	Jack Nicklaus	279
1985	Bernhard Langer	282
1984	Ben Crenshaw	277
1983	Seve Ballesteros	280
1982	Craig Stadler	284
1981	Tom Watson	280
1980	Seve Ballesteros	275
1979	Fuzzy Zoeller	280
1978	Gary Player	277
1977	Tom Watson	276
1976	Ray Floyd	271
1975	Jack Nicklaus	276
1974	Gary Player	278
1973	Tommy Aaron	283
1972	Jack Nicklaus	286
1971	Charles Coody	279
1970	Billy Casper	279
1969	George Archer	281

Year	Winner	Score
1968	Bob Goalby	277
1967	Gay Brewer Jr.	280
1966	Jack Nicklaus	288
1965	Jack Nicklaus	271
1964	Arnold Palmer	276
1963	Jack Nicklaus	286
1962	Arnold Palmer	280
1961	Gary Player	280
1960	Arnold Palmer	282
1959	Art Wall Jr.	284
1958	Arnold Palmer	284
1957	Doug Ford	282
1956	Jack Burke Jr.	289
1955	Cary Middlecoff	279
1954	Sam Snead	289
1953	Ben Hogan	274
1952	Sam Snead	286
1951	Ben Hogan	280
1950	Jimmy Demaret	283
1949	Sam Snead	282
1948	Claude Harmon	279
1947	Jimmy Demaret	281
1946	Herman Keiser	282
1945	No championship played	
1944	No championship played	
1943	No championship played	
1942	Byron Nelson	280
1941	Craig Wood	280
1940	Jimmy Demaret	280
1939	Ralph Guldahl	279
1938	Henry Picard	285
1937	Byron Nelson	283
1936	Horton Smith	285
1935	Gene Sarazen	282
1934	Horton Smith	284

British Open Champions

Year	Winner	Tournament Site
2000	Tiger Woods	St. Andrews, Scotland
1999	Paul Lawrie	Carnoustie, Scotland
1998	Mark O'Meara	Royal Birkdale, England
1997	Justin Leonard	Royal Troon, Scotland
1996	Tom Lehman	Royal Lytham and St. Annes, Lytham, England
1995	John Daly	St. Andrews, Scotland
1994	Nick Price	Turnberry Golf Links' Aisla Course, Scotland
1993	Greg Norman	Royal St. George's, England
1992	Nick Faldo	Muirfield, Scotland
1991	Ian Baker-Finch	Royal Birkdale, England
1990	Nick Faldo	St. Andrews, Scotland
1989	Mark Calcavecchia	Royal Troon, Scotland
1988	Seve Ballesteros	Royal Lytham, England
1987	Nick Faldo	Muirfield, Scotland
1986	Greg Norman	Turnberry, Scotland
1985	Sandy Lyle	Royal St. George's, England
1984	Seve Ballesteros	St. Andrews, Scotland
1983	Tom Watson	Royal Birkdale, England
1982	Tom Watson	Royal Troon, Scotland
1981	Bill Rogers	Royal St. George's, England
1980	Tom Watson	Muirfield, Scotland
1979	Seve Ballesteros	Royal Lytham, England
1978	Jack Nicklaus	St. Andrews, Scotland
1977	Tom Watson	Turnberry, Scotland
1976	Johnny Miller	Royal Birkdale, England
1975	Tom Watson	Carnoustie, Scotland
1974	Gary Player	Royal Lytham, Scotland
1973	Tom Weiskopf	Royal Troon, Scotland
1972	Lee Trevino	Muirfield, Scotland
1971	Lee Trevino	Royal Birkdale, England
1970	Jack Nicklaus	St. Andrews, Scotland
1969	Tony Jacklin	Royal Lytham, Scotland
1968	Gary Player	Carnoustie, Scotland
1967	Roberto Devicenzo	Hoylake, England
1966	Jack Nicklaus	Muirfield, Scotland
1965	Peter Thomson	Southport, England
1964	Tony Lema	St. Andrews, Scotland
1963	Bob Charles	Royal Lytham, England
1962	Arnold Palmer	Royal Troon, Scotland
1961	Arnold Palmer	Royal Birkdale, England
1960	Kel Nagle	St. Andrews, Scotland
1959	Gary Player	Muirfield, Scotland
1958	Peter Thomson	Royal Lytham, England
1957	Bobby Locke	St. Andrews, Scotland
1956	Peter Thomson	Hoylake, England
1955	Peter Thomson	St. Andrews, Scotland
1954	Peter Thomson	Royal Birkdale, England
1953	Ben Hogan	Carnoustie, Scotland
1952	Bobby Locke	Royal Lytham, England
1951	Max Faulkner	Portrush, Ireland
1950	Bobby Locke	Troon, Scotland
1949	Bobby Locke	Royal St. George's, England
1948	Henry Cotton	Muirfield, Scotland
1947	Fred Daly	Hoylake, England
1946	Sam Snead	St. Andrews, Scotland
1945	No championship played	
1944	No championship played	
1943	No championship played	
1942	No championship played	
1941	No championship played	
1940	No championship played	
1939	Richard Burton	St. Andrews, Scotland
1938	R. A. Whitcombe	Royal St. George's, England
1937	Henry Cotton	Carnoustie, Scotland
1936	Alfred Padgham	Hoylake, Scotland
1935	Alfred Perry	Muirfield, Scotland
1934	Henry Cotton	Royal St. George's, England
1933	Denny Shute	St. Andrews, Scotland
1932	Gene Sarazen	Prince's, England
1931	Tommy Armour	Carnoustie, Scotland
1930	Robert Jones Jr.	Hoylake, England
1929	Walter Hagen	Muirfield, Scotland
1928	Walter Hagen	Royal St. George's, England
1927	Bobby Jones	St. Andrews, Scotland
1926	Bobby Jones	Royal Lytham, England
1925	James Barnes	Prestwick, Scotland
1924	Walter Hagen	Hoylake, England
1923	Arthur Havers	Royal Troon, Scotland
1922	Walter Hagen	Royal St. George's, Scotland
1921	Jock Hitchison	St. Andrews, Scotland
1920	George Duncan	Deal, England
1919	No championship played	
1918	No championship played	
1917	No championship played	
1916	No championship played	
1915	No championship played	
1914	Harry Vardon	Prestwick, Scotland
1913	J. H. Taylor	Hoylake, Scotland
1912	Edward Ray	Muirfield, Scotland
1911	Harry Vardon	Royal St. George's, England
1910	James Braid	St. Andrews, Scotland
1909	J. H. Taylor	Deal, England

Year	Winner	Tournament Site
1908	James Braid	Prestwick, Scotland
1907	Arnaud Massy	Hoylake, England
1906	James Braid	Muirfield, Scotland
1905	James Braid	St. Andrews, Scotland
1904	Jack White	Royal St. George's, England
1903	Harry Vardon	Prestwick, Scotland
1902	Alexander Herd	Hoylake, England
1901	James Braid	Muirfield, Scotland
1900	J. H. Taylor	St. Andrews, Scotland
1899	Harry Vardon	Royal St. George's, England
1898	Harry Vardon	Prestwick, Scotland
1897	Harold Hilton	Hoylake, England
1896	Harry Vardon	Muirfield, Scotland
1895	J. H. Taylor	St. Andrews, Scotland
1894	J. H. Taylor	Royal St. George's, England
1893	Wm. Auchterlonie	Prestwick, Scotland
1892	Harold Hilton	Muirfield, Scotland
1891	Hugh Kirkaldy	St. Andrews, Scotland
1890	John Ball	Prestwick, Scotland
1889	Willie Park Jr.	Musselburgh, Scotland
1888	Jack Burns	St. Andrews, Scotland
1887	Willie Park Jr.	Prestwick, Scotland
1886	David Brown	Musselburgh, Scotland
1885	Bob Martin	St. Andrews, Scotland
1884	Jack Simpson	Prestwick, Scotland
1883	Willie Fernie	Musselburgh, Scotland
1882	Robert Ferguson	St. Andrews, Scotland
1881	Robert Ferguson	Prestwick, Scotland
1880	Robert Ferguson	Musselburgh, Scotland
1879	Jamie Anderson	St. Andrews, Scotland
1878	Jamie Anderson	Prestwick, Scotland
1877	Jamie Anderson	Musselburgh, Scotland
1876	Robert Martin	St. Andrews, Scotland
1875	Willie Park	Prestwick, Scotland
1874	Mungo Park	Musselburgh, Scotland
1873	Tom Kidd	St. Andrews, Scotland
1872	Tom Morris Jr.	Prestwick, Scotland
1871	No championship played	
1870	Tom Morris Jr.	Prestwick, Scotland
1869	Tom Morris Jr.	Prestwick, Scotland
1868	Tom Morris Jr.	Prestwick, Scotland
1867	Tom Morris Sr.	Prestwick, Scotland
1866	Willie Park	Prestwick, Scotland
1865	Andrew Strath	Prestwick, Scotland
1864	Tom Morris Sr.	Prestwick, Scotland
1863	Willie Park	Prestwick, Scotland
1862	Tom Morris Sr.	Prestwick, Scotland
1861	Tom Morris Sr.	Prestwick, Scotland
1860	Willie Park	Prestwick, Scotland

U.S. Open Men's Champions

Key	
CC	Country Club
GC	Golf Course
GL	Golf Links

Year	Winner	Tournament Site
2000	Tiger Woods	Pebble Beach GL, Pebble Beach, California
1999	Payne Stewart	Pinehurst Resort and CC, Pinehurst, North Carolina
1998	Lee Janzen	The Olympic Club, San Francisco
1997	Ernie Els	Congressional CC, Bethesda, Maryland
1996	Steve Jones	Oakland Hills CC, Birmingham, Michigan
1995	Corey Pavin	Shinnecock Hills GC, Southampton, New York
1994	Ernie Els	Oakmont CC, Oakmont, Pennsylvania
1993	Lee Janzen	Baltusrol GC, Springfield, New Jersey
1992	Tom Kite	Pebble Beach GL, Pebble Beach, California
1991	Payne Stewart	Hazeltine National GC, Chaska, Minnesota
1990	Hale Irwin	Medinah CC, Medinah, Illinois
1989	Curtis Strange	Oak Hill CC, Rochester, New York
1988	Curtis Strange	The Country Club, Brookline, Massachusetts
1987	Scott Simpson	The Olympic Club, San Francisco
1986	Ray Floyd	Shinnecock Hills GC, Southampton, New York
1985	Andy North	Oakland Hills GC, Birmingham, Michigan
1984	Fuzzy Zoeller	Winged Foot GC, Mamaroneck, New York
1983	Larry Nelson	Oakmont CC, Oakmont, Pennsylvania
1982	Tom Watson	Pebble Beach GL, Pebble Beach, California
1981	David Graham	Merion GC, Ardmore, Pennsylvania

Year	Winner	Tournament Site
1980	Jack Nicklaus	Baltusrol GC, Springfield, New Jersey
1979	Hale Irwin	Inverness Club, Toledo, Ohio
1978	Andy North	Cherry Hills CC, Englewood, Colorado
1977	Hubert Green	Southern Hills CC, Tulsa, Oklahoma
1976	Jerry Pate	Atlanta AC, Duluth, Georgia
1975	Lou Graham	Medinah CC, Medinah, Illinois
1974	Hale Irwin	Winged Foot GC, Mamaroneck, New York
1973	Johnny Miller	Oakmont CC, Oakmont, Pennsylvania
1972	Jack Nicklaus	Pebble Beach GL, Pebble Beach, California
1971	Lee Trevino	Merion GC, Ardmore, Pennsylvania
1970	Tony Jacklin	Hazeltine National GC, Chaska, Minnesota
1969	Orville Moody	Champion GC, Houston
1968	Lee Trevino	Oak Hill CC, Rochester, New York
1967	Jack Nicklaus	Baltusrol GC, Springfield, New Jersey
1966	Billy Casper	The Olympic Club, San Francisco
1965	Gary Player	Bellerive CC, St. Louis
1964	Ken Venturi	Congressional CC, Bethesda, Maryland
1963	Julius Boros	The Country Club, Brookline, Massachusetts
1962	Jack Nicklaus	Oakmont CC, Oakmont, Pennsylvania
1961	Gene Littler	Oakland Hills CC, Birmingham, Michigan
1960	Arnold Palmer	Cherry Hills CC, Englewood, Colorado
1959	Billy Casper	Winged Foot GC, Mamaroneck, New York
1958	Tommy Bolt	Southern Hills CC, Tulsa, Oklahoma
1957	Dick Mayer	Inverness Club, Toledo, Ohio
1956	Cary Middlecoff	Oak Hill CC, Rochester, New York
1955	Jack Fleck	The Olympic Club, San Francisco
1954	Ed Furgol	Baltusrol GC, Springfield, New Jersey
1953	Ben Hogan	Oakmont CC, Oakmont, Pennsylvania
1952	Julius Boros	Northwood Club, Dallas
1951	Ben Hogan	Oakland Hills CC, Birmingham, Michigan
1950	Ben Hogan	Merion GC, Ardmore, Pennsylvania
1949	Cary Middlecoff	Medinah CC, Medinah, Illinois
1948	Ben Hogan	Riviera CC, Los Angeles
1947	Lew Worsham	St. Louis CC, Clayton, Missouri
1946	Lloyd Mangrum	Canterbury GC, Cleveland
1942–1945		No championship played
1941	Craig Wood	Colonial CC, Fort Worth, Texas
1940	Lawson Little	Canterbury GC, Cleveland
1939	Byron Nelson	Philadelphia CC, Philadelphia
1938	Ralph Guldahl	Cherry Hills CC, Englewood, Colorado
1937	Ralph Guldahl	Oakland Hills CC, Birmingham, Michigan
1936	Tony Manero	Baltusrol GC, Springfield, New Jersey
1935	Sam Parks Jr.	Oakmont CC, Oakmont, Pennsylvania
1934	Olin Dutra	Merion GC, Ardmore, Pennsylvania
1933	Johnny Goodman	North Shore GC, Glenview, Illinois
1932	Gene Sarazen	Fresh Meadow CC, Flushing, New York
1931	Billy Burke	Inverness Club, Toledo, Ohio
1930	Bobby Jones	Interlachen CC, Minneapolis
1929	Bobby Jones	Winged Foot GC, Mamaroneck, New York
1928	Johnny Farrell	Olympic Field GC, Matteson, Illinois
1927	Tommy Armour	Oakmont CC, Oakmont, Pennsylvania
1926	Bobby Jones	Scioto CC, Columbus, Ohio
1925	Willie MacFarlane	Worcester CC, Worcester, Massachusetts
1924	Cyril Walker	Oakland Hills CC, Birmingham, Michigan

Year	Winner	Tournament Site
1923	Bobby Jones	Inwood CC Inwood, New York
1922	Gene Sarazen	Skokie GC, Glencoe, Illinois
1921	James Barnes	Columbia CC, Chevy Chase, Maryland
1920	Edward Ray	Inverness Club, Toledo, Ohio
1919	Walter Hagen	Brae Burn CC, West Newton, Massachusetts
1917–1918		No championship played
1916	Charles Evans Jr.	Minikahda Club, Minneapolis
1915	Jerome Travers	Baltusrol GC, Springfield, New Jersey
1914	Walter Hagen	Midlothian CC, Blue Island, Illinois
1913	Francis Ouimet	The Country Club, Brookline, Massachusetts
1912	John McDermott	CC of Buffalo Buffalo, New York
1911	John McDermott	Chicago GC, Wheaton, Illinois
1910	Alex Smith	Philadelphia Cricket Club, Philadelphia
1909	George Sargent	Englewood GC, Englewood, New Jersey
1908	Fred McLeod	Myopia Hunt Club, Hamilton, Massachusetts
1907	Alex Ross	Philadelphia Cricket Club, Philadelphia
1906	Alex Smith	Onwentsia Club, Lake Forest, Illinois
1905	Willie Anderson	Myopia Hunt Club, Hamilton, Massachusetts
1904	Willie Anderson	Glen View Club, Golf, Illinois
1903	Willie Anderson	Baltusrol GC, Springfield, New Jersey
1902	Laurie Auchterlonie	Garden City GC, Garden City, New York
1901	Willie Anderson	Myopia Hunt Club, Hamilton, Massachusetts
1900	Harry Vardon	Chicago GC, Wheaton, Illinois
1899	Willie Smith	Baltimore CC, Baltimore
1898	Fred Herd	Myopia Hunt Club, Hamilton, Massachusetts
1897	Joe Lloyd	Chicago GC, Wheaton, Illinois
1896	James Foulis	Shinnecock Hills GC, Southampton, New York
1895	Horace Rawlins	Newport GC, Newport, Rhode Island

PGA Champions

Year	Winner	Tournament Site
2000	Tiger Woods	Valhalla, Louisville, Kentucky
1999	Tiger Woods	Medinah, Medinah, Illinois
1998	Vijay Singh	Sahalee, Redmond, Washington
1997	Davis Love III	Winged Foot, Mamaroneck, New York
1996	Mark Brooks	Valhalla, Louisville, Kentucky
1995	Steve Elkington	Riviera, Los Angeles
1994	Nick Price	Southern Hills, Tulsa, Oklahoma
1993	Paul Azinger	Inverness, Toledo, Ohio
1992	Nick Price	Bellerive, St. Louis
1991	John Daly	Crooked Stick, Carmel, Indiana
1990	Wayne Grady	Shoal Creek, Birmingham, Alabama
1989	Payne Stewart	Kemper Lakes, Hawthorn Woods, Illinois
1988	Jeff Sluman	Oak Tree, Edmond, Oklahoma
1987	Larry Nelson	PGA National, Palm Beach Gardens, Florida
1986	Bob Tway	Inverness, Toledo, Ohio
1985	Hubert Green	Cherry Hills, Englewood, Colorado
1984	Lee Trevino	Shoal Creek, Birmingham, Alabama
1983	Hal Sutton	Riviera, Pacific Palisades, California
1982	Raymond Floyd	Southern Hills, Tulsa, Oklahoma
1981	Larry Nelson	Atlanta Athletic Club, Duluth, Georgia
1980	Jack Nicklaus	Oak Hill, Rochester, New York
1979	David Graham	Oakland Hills, Birmingham, Michigan
1978	John Mahaffey	Oakmont, Oakmont, Pennsylvania
1977	Lanny Wadkins	Pebble Beach, Pebble Beach, California
1976	Dave Stockton	Congressional, Bethesda, Maryland
1975	Jack Nicklaus	Firestone, Akron, Ohio

Year	Winner	Tournament Site
1974	Lee Trevino	Tanglewood, Winston-Salem, North Carolina
1973	Jack Nicklaus	Canterbury, Cleveland
1972	Gary Player	Oakland Hills, Birmingham, Michigan
1971	Jack Nicklaus	PGA National, Palm Beach Gardens, Florida
1970	Dave Stockton	Southern Hills, Tulsa, Oklahoma
1969	Ray Floyd	NCR, Dayton, Ohio
1968	Julius Boros	Pecan Valley, San Antonio, Texas
1967	Don January	Columbine, Littleton, Colorado
1966	Al Geiberger	Firestone, Akron, Ohio
1965	Dave Marr	Laurel Valley, Ligonier, Pennsylvania
1964	Bobby Nichols	Columbus, Columbus, Ohio
1963	Jack Nicklaus	Dallas Athletic Club, Dallas
1962	Gary Player	Aronomink, Newtown Square, Pennsylvania
1961	Jerry Barber	Olympia Fields, Olympia Fields, Illinois
1960	Jay Hebert	Firestone, Akron, Ohio
1959	Bob Rosburg	Minneapolis, St. Louis Park, Minnesota
1958	Dow Finsterwald	Llanerch, Havertown, Pennsylvania
1957	Lionel Hebert	Miami Valley, Dayton, Ohio
1956	Jack Burke	Blue Hill, Boston
1955	Doug Ford	Meadowbrook, Detroit
1954	Chick Harbert	Keller, St. Paul, Minnesota
1953	Walter Burkemo	Birmingham, Birmingham, Michigan
1952	Jim Turnesa	Big Spring, Louisville, Kentucky
1951	Sam Snead	Oakmont, Oakmont, Pennsylvania
1950	Chandler Harper	Scioto, Columbus, Ohio
1949	Sam Snead	Hermitage, Richmond, Virginia
1948	Ben Hogan	Norwood Hills, St. Louis
1947	Jim Ferrier	Plum Hollow, Detroit
1946	Ben Hogan	Portland, Portland, Oregon
1945	Byron Nelson	Morraine, Dayton, Ohio
1944	Bob Hamilton	Manito, Spokane, Washington

Year	Winner	Tournament Site
1943	No championship played	
1942	Sam Snead	Seaview, Atlantic City, New Jersey
1941	Vic Ghezzi	Cherry Hills, Engelwood, Colorado
1940	Byron Nelson	Hershey, Hershey, Pennsylvania
1939	Henry Picard	Pomonok, Flushing, New York
1938	Paul Runyan	Shawnee, Shawnee-on-Delaware, Pennsylvania
1937	Denny Shute	Pittsburgh, Aspinwall, Pennsylvania
1936	Denny Shute	Pinehurst, Pinehurst, North Carolina
1935	Johnny Revolta	Twin Hills, Oklahoma City, Oklahoma
1934	Paul Runyan	Park, Williamsville, New York
1933	Gene Sarazen	Blue Mound, Milwaukee
1932	Olin Dutra	Keller, St. Paul, Minnesota
1931	Tom Creavy	Wannamoisett, Rumford, Rhode Island
1930	Tommy Armour	Fresh Meadow, Flushing, New York
1929	Leo Diegel	Hillcrest, Los Angeles
1928	Leo Diegel	Five Farms, Baltimore
1927	Walter Hagen	Cedar Crest, Dallas
1926	Walter Hagen	Salisbury, Westbury, New York
1925	Walter Hagen	Olympia Fields, Olympia Fields, Illinois
1924	Walter Hagen	French Lick, French Lick, Indiana
1923	Gene Sarazen	Pelham, Pelham, New York
1922	Gene Sarazen	Oakmont, Oakmont, Pennsylvania
1921	Walter Hagen	Inwood, Far Rockaway, New York
1920	Jock Hutchison	Flossmoor, Flossmoor, Illinois
1919	James Barnes	Engineers', Roslyn, New York
1918	No championship played	
1917	No championship played	
1916	James Barnes	Siwanoy, Bronxville, New York

Men's U.S. Amateur

36-Hole Stroke Play Qualifying Before Match Play 1979–Present

1999: David Gossett defeated Sung Yoon Kim, Pebble Beach Golf Links, Pebble Beach, Calif.

1998: Hank Kuehne defeated Tom McKnight, Oak Hill Country Club (East Course), Rochester, N.Y.

1997: Matthew Kuchar defeated Joel Kribel, Cog Hill Golf and Country Club (No. 4 Course), Lemont, Ill.

1996: Tiger Woods defeated Steve Scott, Pumpkin Ridge Golf Club, North Plains, Ore.

1995: Tiger Woods defeated George "Buddy" Marucci Jr., Newport Country Club, Newport, R.I.

1994: Tiger Woods defeated Trip Kuehne, TPC at Sawgrass (Stadium Course), Ponte Vedra, Fla.

1993: John Harris defeated Danny Ellis, Champions Golf Club (Cypress Creek Course), Houston, Tex.

1992: Justin Leonard defeated Tom Scherrer, Muirfield Village Golf Club, Dublin, Ohio.

1991: Mitch Voges defeated Manny Zerman, The Honors Course, Chattanooga, Tenn.

1990: Phil Mickelson defeated Manny Zerman, Cherry Hills Country Club, Englewood, Colo.

1989: Chris Patton defeated Danny Green, Merion Golf Club (East Course), Ardmore, Pa.

1988: Eric Meeks defeated Danny Yates, Virginia Hot Springs Golf & Country Club (Cascades Course), Hot Springs, Va.

1987: Billy Mayfair defeated Eric Rebmann, Jupiter Hills Club (Hills Course), Jupiter, Fla.

1986: Buddy Alexander defeated Chris Kite, Shoal Creek, Birmingham, Ala.

1985: Sam Randolph defeated Peter Persons, Montclair Golf Club, West Orange, N.J.

1984: Scott Verplank defeated Sam Randolph, Oak Tree Golf Club, Edmond, Okla.

1983: Jay Sigel defeated Chris Perry, North Shore Country Club, Glenview, Ill.

1982: Jay Sigel defeated David Tolley, The Country Club, Brookline, Mass.

1981: Nathaniel Crosby defeated Brian Lindley, Olympic Club (Lake Course), San Francisco, Calif.

1980: Hal Sutton defeated Bob Lewis, Country Club of North Carolina, Pinehurst, N.C.

1979: Mark O'Meara defeated John Cook, Canterbury Golf Club, Cleveland, Ohio.

All Match Play 1973–1978

1978: John Cook defeated Scott Hoch, Plainfield Country Club, Plainfield, N.J.

1977: John Fought defeated Doug Fischesser, Aronimink Golf Club, Newtown Square, Pa.

1976: Bill Sander defeated C. Parker Moore Jr., Bel-Air Country Club, Los Angeles, Calif.

1975: Fred Ridley defeated Keith Fergus, Country Club of Virginia (James River Course), Richmond, Va.

1974: Jerry Pate defeated John P. Grace, Ridgewood Country Club, Ridgewood, N.J.

1973: Craig Stadler defeated David Strawn, Inverness Club, Toledo, Ohio.

All Stroke Play 1965–1972

1972: Marvin Giles III, 285; Mark S. Hayes, 288; Ben Crenshaw, 288; Charlotte Country Club, Charlotte, N.C.

1971: Gary Cowan, 280; Eddie Pearce, 283; Wilmington Country Club (South Course), Wilmington, Del.

1970: Lanny Wadkins, 279; Thomas O. Kite Jr., 280; Waverley Country Club, Portland, Ore.

1969: Steven N. Melnyk, 286; Marvin Giles III, 291; Oakmont Country Club, Oakmont, Pa.

1968: Bruce Fleisher, 284; Marvin Giles III, 285; Scioto Country Club, Columbus, Ohio.

1967: Robert B. Dickson, 285; Marvin Giles III, 286; Broadmoor Golf Club (West Course), Colorado Springs, Colo.

1966: Gary Cowan 285; Deane Beman, 285; Merion Golf Club (East Course), Ardmore, Pa.

1965: Robert J. Murphy Jr., 291; Robert B. Dickson, 292; Southern Hills Country Club, Tulsa, Okla.

All Match Play 1947–1964

1964: William C. Campbell defeated Edgar M. Tutwiler, Canterbury Golf Club, Cleveland, Ohio.

1963: Deane Beman defeated Richard H. Sikes, Wakonda Club, Des Moines, Iowa.

1962: Labron E. Harris Jr. defeated Downing Gray, Pinehurst Country Club (No. 2 Course), Pinehurst, N.C.

1961: Jack Nicklaus defeated H. Dudley Wysong Jr., Pebble Beach Golf Links, Pebble Beach, Calif.

1960: Deane Beman defeated Robert W. Gardner, St. Louis Country Club, Clayton, Mo.

1959: Jack Nicklaus defeated Charles R. Coe, Broadmoor Golf Club (East Course), Colorado Springs.

1958: Charles R. Coe defeated Thomas D. Aaron, Olympic Club (Lake Course), San Francisco, Calif.

1957: Hillman Robbins Jr. defeated Dr. Frank M. Taylor, The Country Club (Anniversary Course), Brookline, Mass.

1956: E. Harvie Ward Jr. defeated Charles Kocsis, Knollwood Club, Lake Forest, Ill.

1955: E. Harvie Ward Jr. defeated William Hyndman Jr., Country Club of Virginia (James River Course), Richmond, Va.

1954: Arnold Palmer defeated Robert Sweeny, Country Club of Detroit, Grosse Pointe Farms, Mich.

1953: Gene Littler defeated Dale Morey, Oklahoma City Golf & Country Club, Oklahoma City, Okla.

1952: Jack Westland defeated Al Mengert, Seattle Golf Club, Seattle, Wash.

1951: Billy Maxwell defeated Joseph F. Gagliardi, Saucon Valley Country Club (Old Course), Bethlehem, Pa.

1950: Sam Urzetta defeated Frank Stranahan, Minneapolis Golf Club, Minn.

1949: Charles R. Coe defeated Rufus King, Oak Hill Country Club (East Course), Rochester, N.Y.

1948: William P. Turnesa defeated Raymond E. Billows, Memphis Country Club, Memphis, Tenn.

1947: Robert H. "Skee" Riegel defeated John W. Dawson, Del Monte Golf & Country Club (Pebble Beach Golf Links), Pebble Beach, Calif.

1946: Stanley E. (Ted) Bishop defeated Smiley L. Quick, Baltusrol Golf Club (Lower Course), Springfield, N.J.

1942–45: No championships played

1941: Marvin H. Ward defeated B. Patrick Abbott, Omaha Field Club, Omaha, Neb.

1940: Richard D. Chapman defeated W. B. McCullough Jr., Winged Foot Golf Club (West Course), Mamaroneck, N.Y.

1939: Marvin H. Ward defeated Raymond E. Billows, North Shore Country Club, Glenview, Ill.

1938: William P. Turnesa defeated B. Patrick Abbott, Oakmont Country Club, Oakmont, Pa.

1937: John Goodman defeated Raymond E. Billows, Alderwood Country Club, Portland, Ore.

1936: John W. Fischer defeated Jack McLean, Garden City Golf Club, Garden City, N.Y.

1935: W. Lawson Little Jr. defeated Walter Emery, The Country Club, Cleveland, Ohio.

1934: W. Lawson Little Jr. defeated David Goldman, The Country Club, Brookline, Mass.

1933: George T. Dunlap Jr. defeated Max R. Marston, Kenwood Country Club, Cincinnati.

1932: C. Ross Somerville defeated John Goodman, Baltimore Country Club (Five Farms East Course), Timonium, Md.

1931: Francis Ouimet defeated Jack Westland, Beverly Country Club, Chicago, Ill.

1930: Bobby Jones defeated Eugene V. Homans, Merion Cricket Club (East Course), Ardmore, Pa.

1929: Harrison R. Johnston defeated Dr. O. F. Willing, Del Monte Golf & Country Club (Pebble Beach Golf Links), Pebble Beach, Calif.

1928: Bobby Jones defeated T. Phillip Perkins, Brae Burn Country Club, West Newton, Mass.

1927: Bobby Jones defeated Charles Evans, Jr., Minikahda Club, Minneapolis, Minn.

1926: George Von Elm defeated Robert T. Jones Jr., Baltusrol Golf Club (Lower Course), Springfield, N.J.

1925: Bobby Jones defeated Watts Gunn, Oakmont Country Club, Oakmont, Pa.

1924: Bobby Jones defeated George Von Elm, Merion Cricket Club (East Course), Ardmore, Pa.

1923: Max R. Marston defeated Jess W. Sweetser, Flossmoor Country Club, Flossmoor, Ill.

1922: Jess W. Sweetser defeated Charles Evans Jr., The Country Club, Brookline, Mass.

1921: Jesse P. Guilford defeated Robert A. Gardner, St. Louis Country Club, Clayton, Mo.

1920: Charles Evans Jr. defeated Francis Ouimet, Engineers' Country Club, Roslyn, N.Y.

1919: S. Davidson Herron defeated Bobby Jones, Oakmont Country Club, Oakmont, Pa.

1917–18: No championships played

1916: Charles Evans Jr. defeated Robert A. Gardner, Merion Cricket Club (East Course), Haverford, Pa.

1915: Robert A. Gardner defeated John G. Anderson, Country Club of Detroit, Grosse Pointe Farms, Mich.

1914: Francis Ouimet defeated Jerome D. Travers, Ekwanok Country Club, Manchester, Vt.

1913: Jerome D. Travers defeated John G. Anderson, Garden City Golf Club, Garden City, N.Y.

1912: Jerome D. Travers defeated Charles Evans Jr., Chicago Golf Club, Wheaton, Ill.

1911: Harold H. Hilton defeated Fred Herreshoff, The Apawamis Club, Rye, N.Y.

1910: William C. Fownes Jr. defeated Warren K. Wood, The Country Club, Brookline, Mass.

1909: Robert A. Gardner defeated H. Chandler Egan, Chicago Golf Club, Wheaton, Ill.

1908: Jerome D. Travers defeated Max H. Behr, Garden City Golf Club, Garden City, N.Y.

1907: Jerome D. Travers defeated Archibald Graham, Euclid Club, Cleveland, Ohio.

1906: Eben M. Byers defeated George S. Lyon, Englewood Golf Club, Englewood, N.J.

1905: H. Chandler Egan defeated D. E. Sawyer, Chicago Golf Club, Wheaton, Ill.

1904: H. Chandler Egan defeated Fred Herreshoff, Baltusrol Golf Club (original course), Springfield, N.J.

1903: Walter J. Travis defeated Eben M. Byers, Nassau Country Club, Glen Cove, N.Y.

1902: Louis N. James defeated Eben M. Byers, Glen View Club, Golf, Ill.

1901: Walter J. Travis defeated Walter E. Egan, Country Club of Atlantic City, Atlantic City, N.J.

1900: Walter J. Travis defeated Findlay S. Douglas, Garden City Golf Club. Garden City, N.Y.

1899: H. M. Harriman defeated Findlay S. Douglas, Onwentsia Club, Lake Forest, Ill.

1898: Findlay S. Douglas defeated Walter B. Smith, Morris County Golf Club, Morristown, N.J.

1897: H. J. Whigham defeated W. Rossiter Betts, Chicago Golf Club, Wheaton, Ill.

1896: H. J. Whigham defeated J. G. Thorp, Shinnecock Hills Golf Club, Southampton, N.Y.

1895: Charles B. Macdonald defeated Charles E. Sands, Newport Golf Club, Newport, R.I.

The U.S. Women's Amateur

1999: Dorothy Delasin defeated Jimin Kang, Biltmore Forest Country Club, Asheville, N.C.

1998: Grace Park defeated Jenny Chuasiriporn, Barton Hills Country Club, Ann Arbor, Mich.

1997: Silvia Cavalleri defeated Robin Burke, Brae Burn Country Club, West Newton, Mass.

1996: Kelli Kuehne defeated Marisa Baena, Firethorn Golf Club, Lincoln, Neb.

1995: Kelli Kuehne defeated Anne–Marie Knight, The Country Club, Brookline, Mass.

1994: Wendy Ward defeated Jill McGill, The Homestead (Cascades Course), Hot Springs, Va.

1993: Jill McGill defeated Sarah LeBrun Ingram, San Diego Country Club, Chula Vista, Calif.

1992: Vicki Goetze defeated Annika Sorenstam, Kemper Lakes Golf Club, Long Grove, Ill.

1991: Amy Fruhwirth defeated Heidi Voorhees, Prairie Dunes Country Club, Hutchinson, Kans.

1990: Pat Hurst defeated Stephanie Davis, Canoe Brook Country Club (North Course), Summit, N.J.

1989: Vicki Goetze defeated Brandie Burton, Pinehurst Country Club (No. 2), Pinehurst, N.C.

1988: Pearl Sinn defeated Karen Noble, Minikahda Club, Minneapolis, Minn.

1987: Kay Cockerill defeated Tracy Kerdyk, Rhode Island Country Club, Barrington, R.I.

1986: Kay Cockerill defeated Kathleen McCarthy, Pasatiempo Golf Club, Santa Cruz, Calif.

1985: Michiko Hattori defeated Cheryl Stacy, Fox Chapel Country Club, Pittsburgh, Pa.

1984: Deb Richard defeated Kimberly Williams, Broadmoor Golf Club, Seattle, Wash.

1983: Joanne Pacillo defeated Sally Quinlan, Canoe Brook Country Club (North Course), Summit, N.J.

1982: Juli Simpson Inkster defeated Cathy Hanlon, Broadmoor Golf Club, (South Course), Colorado Springs, Colo.

1981: Juli Simpson Inkster defeated Lindy Goggin, Waverley Country Club, Portland, Ore.

1980: Juli Simpson Inkster defeated Patti Rizzo, Prairie Dunes Country Club, Hutchinson, Kans.

1979: Carolyn Hill defeated Patty Sheehan, Memphis Country Club, Memphis, Tenn.

1978: Cathy Sherk defeated Judith Oliver, Sunnybrook Golf Club, Plymouth Meeting, Pa.

1977: Beth Daniel defeated Cathy Sherk, Cincinnati Country Club, Cincinnati, Ohio.

1976: Donna Horton defeated Marianne Bretton, Del Paso Country Club, Sacramento, Calif.

1975: Beth Daniel defeated Donna Horton, Brae Burn Country Club, West Newton, Mass.

1974: Cynthia Hill defeated Carol Semple, Broadmoor Golf Club, Seattle, Wash.

1973: Carol Semple defeated Anne Quast Sander, Montclair Golf Club, Montclair, N.J.

1972: Mary Budke defeated Cynthia Hill, St. Louis Country Club, St. Louis, Mo.

1971: Laura Baugh defeated Beth Barry, Atlanta Country Club, Atlanta, Ga.

1970: Martha Wilkinson defeated Cynthia Hill, Wee Burn Country Club, Darien, Conn.

1969: Catherine Lacoste defeated Shelley Hamlin, Las Colinas Country Club, Irving, Tex.

1968: JoAnne Gunderson Carner defeated Anne Quast Sander, Birmingham Country Club, Birmingham, Mich.

1967: Mary Lou Dill defeated Jean Ashley, Annandale Golf Club, Pasadena, Calif.

1966: JoAnne Gunderson defeated Marlene Stewart Streit, Sewickley Heights Golf Club, Sewickley, Pa.

1965: Jean Ashley defeated Anne Quast Sander, Lakewood Country Club, Denver, Colo.

1964: Barbara McIntire defeated JoAnne Gunderson, Prairie Dunes Country Club, Hutchinson, Kans.

1963: Anne Quast Sander defeated Peggy Conley, Taconic Golf Club, Williamstown, Mass.

1962: JoAnne Gunderson defeated Ann Baker, Country Club of Rochester, Rochester, N.Y.

1961: Anne Quast Sander defeated Phyllis Preuss, Tacoma Golf and Country Club, Tacoma, Wash.

1960: JoAnne Gunderson defeated Jean Ashley, Tulsa Country Club, Tulsa, Okla.

1959: Barbara McIntire defeated Joanne Goodwin, Congressional Country Club, Washington, D.C.

1958: Anne Quast defeated Barbara Romack, Wee Burn Country Club, Darien, Conn.

1957: JoAnne Gunderson defeated Ann Casey Johnstone, Del Paso Country Club, Sacramento, Calif.

1956: Marlene Stewart defeated JoAnne Gunderson, Meridian Hills Country Club, Indianapolis, Ind.

1955: Patricia A. Lesser defeated Jane Nelson, Myers Park Country Club, Charlotte, N.C.

1954: Barbara Romack defeated Mickey Wright, Allegheny Country Club, Sewickley, Pa.

1953: Mary Lena Faulk defeated Polly Riley, Rhode Island Country Club, West Barrington, R.I.

1952: Jacqueline Pung defeated Shirley McFedters, Waverley Country Club, Portland, Ore.

1951: Dorothy Kirby defeated Claire Doran, Town & Country Club, St. Paul, Minn.

1950: Beverly Hanson defeated Mae Murray, Atlanta A. C. (East Lake), Atlanta, Ga.

1949: Dorothy Porter defeated Dorothy Kielty, Merion Golf Club (East Course), Ardmore, Pa.

1948: Grace S. Lenczyk defeated Helen Sigel, Del Monte Golf & Country Club (Pebble Beach Golf Links), Pebble Beach, Calif.

1947: Louise Suggs defeated Dorothy Kirby, Franklin Hills Country Club, Franklin, Mich.

1946: Babe Didrikson Zaharias defeated Clara Sherman, Southern Hills Country Club, Tulsa, Okla.

1942–45: No championships played

1941: Elizabeth Hicks defeated Helen Sigel, The Country Club, Brookline, Mass.

1940: Betty Jameson defeated Jane S. Cothran, Del Monte Golf & Country Club (Pebble Beach Golf Links), Pebble Beach, Calif.

1939: Betty Jameson defeated Dorothy Kirby, Wee Burn Club, Darien, Conn.

1938: Patty Berg defeated Estelle Lawson Page, Westmoreland Country Club, Wilmette, Ill.

1937: Estelle Lawson Page defeated Patty Berg, Memphis Country Club, Memphis, Tenn.

1936: Pamela Barton defeated Maureen Orcutt, Canoe Brook Country Club (South Course), Summit, N.J.

1935: Glenna Collett Vare defeated Patty Berg, Interlachen Country Club, Hopkins, Minn.

1934: Virginia Van Wie defeated Dorothy Traung, Whitemarsh Valley Country Club, Chestnut Hill, Pa.

1933: Virginia Van Wie defeated Helen Hicks, Exmoor Country Club, Highland Park, Ill.

1932: Virginia Van Wie defeated Glenna Collett Vare, Salem Country Club, Peabody, Mass.

1931: Helen Hicks defeated Glenna Collet Vare, Country Club of Buffalo, Williamsville, N.Y.

1930: Glenna Collett defeated Virginia Van Wie, Los Angeles Country Club (North Course), Beverly Hills, Calif.

1929: Glenna Collett defeated Leona Pressler, Oakland Hills Country Club (South Course), Birmingham, Mich.

1928: Glenna Collett defeated Virginia Van Wie, Virginia Hot Springs Golf & Tennis Club (Cascades Course), Hot Springs, Va.

1927: Miriam Burns Horn defeated Maureen Orcutt, Cherry Valley Club, Garden City, N.Y.

1926: Helen Stetson defeated Elizabeth Goss, Merion Cricket Club (East Course), Ardmore, Pa.

1925: Glenna Collett defeated Alexa Stirling, St. Louis Country Club, Clayton, Mo.

1924: Dorothy Campbell Hurd defeated Mary K. Browne, Rhode Island Country Club, Nyatt, R.I.

1923: Edith Cummings defeated Alexa Stirling, Westchester Country Club (Original Course), Rye, N.Y.

1922: Glenna Collett defeated Margaret Gavin, Greenbrier Golf Club, White Sulphur Springs, W. Va.

1921: Marion Hollins defeated Alexa Stirling, Hollywood Golf Club, Deal, N.J.

1920: Alexa Stirling defeated Dorothy Campbell Hurd, Mayfield Country Club, Cleveland, Ohio.

1919: Alexa Stirling defeated Margaret Gavin, Shawnee Country Club, Shawnee-on-Delaware, Pa.

1917–18: No championships played

1916: Alexa Stirling defeated Mildred Caverly, Belmont Springs Country Club, Waverley, Mass.

1915: Florence Vanderbeck defeated Margaret Gavin, Onwentsia Club, Lake Forest, Ill.

1914: Katherine C. Harley defeated Elaine V. Rosenthal, Nassau Country Club, Glen Cove, N.Y.

1913: Gladys Ravenscroft defeated Marion Hollins, Wilmington Country Club (Original Course), Wilmington, Del.

1912: Margaret Curtis defeated Nonna Barlow, Essex County Club, Manchester, Mass.

1911: Margaret Curtis defeated Lillian B. Hyde, Baltusrol Golf Club (Original Course), Springfield, N.J.

1910: Dorothy I. Campbell defeated Mrs. G. M. Martin, Homewood Country Club, Flossmoor, Ill.

1909: Dorothy I. Campbell defeated Nonna Barlow, Merion Cricket Club (Original Course), Haverford, Pa.

1908: Katherine C. Harley defeated Mrs. T. H. Polhemus, Chevy Chase Club, Chevy Chase, Md.

1907: Margaret Curtis defeated Harriot S. Curtis, Midlothian Country Club, Blue Island, Ill.

1906: Harriot S. Curtis defeated Mary B. Adams, Brae Burn Country Club, West Newton, Mass.

1905: Pauline Mackay defeated Margaret Curtis, Morris County Golf Club, Convent Station, N.J.

1904: Georgianna M. Bishop defeated Mrs. E. F. Sanford, Merion Cricket Club (Original Course), Haverford, Pa.

1903: Bessie Anthony defeated J. Anna Carpenter, Chicago Golf Club, Wheaton, Ill.

1902: Genevieve Hecker defeated Louisa A. Wells, The Country Club (Original Course) Brookline, Mass.

1901: Genevieve Hecker defeated Lucy Herron, Baltusrol Golf Club (Original Course), Springfield, N.J.

1900: Frances C. Griscom defeated Margaret Curtis, Shinnecock Hills Golf Club, Southampton, N.Y.

1899: Ruth Underhill defeated Margaret Fox, Philadelphia Country Club (Bala Course), Pa.

1898: Beatrix Hoyt defeated Maude Wetmore, Ardsley Club, Ardsley, N.Y.

1897: Beatrix Hoyt defeated Nellie Sargent, Essex County Club, Manchester, Mass.

1896: Beatrix Hoyt defeated Mrs. Arthur Turnure, Morris County Golf Club, Convent Station, N.J.

1895: Mrs. C. S. Brown defeated Nellie Sargent, Meadow Brook Club, Hempstead, N.Y.

Multiple Winners

6	Glenna Collett Vare
5	JoAnne Gunderson Carner
3	Margaret Curtis
	Beatrix Hoyt
	Dorothy Campbell Hurd
	Julie Inkster
	Alexa Stirling
	Virginia Van Wie
	Anne Quast Decker Welts

U.S. Women's Open Winners

Year	Winner	Score
2000	Karrie Webb	282
1999	Julie Inkster	272
1998	Se Ri Pak*	290
1997	Alison Nicholas	274
1996	Annika Sorenstam	272
1995	Annika Sorenstam	278
1994	Patty Sheehan	277
1993	Lauri Merten	280
1992	Patty Sheehan**	280
1991	Meg Mallon	283
1990	Betsy King	284
1989	Betsy King	278
1988	Liselotte Neumann	277
1987	Laura Davies***	285
1986	Jane Geddes****	287
1985	Kathy Baker	280
1984	Hollis Stacy	290
1983	Jan Stephenson	290
1982	Janet Anderson	283
1981	Pat Bradley	279
1980	Amy Alcott	280
1979	Jerilyn Britz	284
1978	Hollis Stacy	289
1977	Hollis Stacy	292
1976	JoAnne Carner*****	292
1975	Sandra Palmer	295
1974	Sandra Haynie	295
1973	Susie M. Berning	290
1972	Susie M. Berning	299

*Pak defeated Jenny Chuasiriporn on the 2nd sudden death hole; they were tied after an 18-hole playoff.

**Sheehan defeated Julie Inkster, 72-74, in 18-hole playoff.

***Davis defeated Ayako Okamoto and JoAnne Carner, 71-73-74, in 18-hole playoff.

****Geddes defeated Sally Little, 71-73, in 18-hole playoff.

*****Carner defeated Sandra Palmer, 76-78, in 18-hole playoff.

Year	Winner	Score		Year	Winner	Score
1971	JoAnne Carner	288		1993	Patty Sheehan	275
1970	Donna Caponi	287		1992	Betsy King	267
1969	Donna Caponi	294		1991	Meg Mallon	274
1968	Susie M. Berning	289		1990	Beth Daniel	280
1967	Catherine Lacoste	294		1989	Nancy Lopez	274
1966	Sandra Spuzich	297		1988	Sherri Turner	281
1965	Carol Mann	290		1987	Jane Geddes	275
1964	Mickey Wright*	290		1986	Pat Bradley	277
1963	Mary Mills	289		1985	Nancy Lopez	273
1962	Murle Lindstrom	301		1984	Patty Sheehan	272
1961	Mickey Wright	293		1983	Patty Sheehan	279
1960	Betsy Rawls	292		1982	Jan Stephenson	279
1959	Mickey Wright	287		1981	Donna Caponi	280
1958	Mickey Wright	290		1980	Sally Little	285
1957	Betsy Rawls	299		1979	Donna Caponi	279
1956	Kathy Cornelius**	302		1978	Nancy Lopez	275
1955	Fay Crocker	299		1977	Chako Higuchi	279
1954	Babe Zaharias	291		1976	Betty Burfeindt	287
1953	Betsy Rawls***	302		1975	Kathy Whitworth	288
1952	Louise Suggs	284		1974	Sandra Haynie	288
1951	Betsy Rawls	293		1973	Mary Mills	288
1950	Babe Zaharias	291		1972	Kathy Ahern	293
1949	Louise Suggs	291		1971	Kathy Whitworth	288
1948	Babe Zaharias	300		1970	Shirley Englehorn	285
1947	Betty Jameson	295		1969	Betsy Rawls	293
1946	Patty Berg	5 & 4		1968	Sandra Post	294
				1967	Kathy Whitworth	284
				1966	Gloria Ehret	282
				1965	Sandra Haynie	279
				1964	Mary Mills	278
				1963	Mickey Wright	294
				1962	Judy Kimball	282
				1961	Mickey Wright	287
				1960	Mickey Wright	292
				1959	Betsy Rawls	288
				1958	Mickey Wright	288
				1957	Louise Suggs	285
				1956	Marlene Hagge	291
				1955	Beverly Hanson	220

*Wright defeated Ruth Jessen, 70-72, in 18-hole playoff.
**Cornelius defeated Barbara McIntire, 75-82, in 18-hole playoff.
***Rawls defeated Jackie Pung, 71-77 in 18-hole playoff.

LPGA Championship
(a women's major pro tournament)

Year	Winner	Score
1999	Julie Inkster	268
1998	Se Ri Pak	273
1997	Chris Johnson	281
1996	Laura Davies	213
1995	Kelly Robbins	274
1994	Laura Davies	279

Notes

Introduction: An Ancient Game Gathers Strength for a New Millennium

1. Arnold Palmer, *My Game and Yours.* New York: Simon and Schuster, 1965, p. 9.
2. Quoted in Jaime Diaz, "Masters Plan," *Sports Illustrated,* April 13, 1998, p. 65.
3. Quoted in Jack Canfield et al., *Chicken Soup for the Golfer's Soul: 101 Stories of Insight, Inspiration and Laughter on the Links.* Deerfield Beach, FL: Health Communications, 1999, p. 116.

Chapter 1: The Early History of Golf

4. Quoted in Webster Evans, *Encyclopaedia of Golf.* New York: St. Martin's Press, 1974, pp. 122–123.
5. Herbert Warren Wind, *The Story of American Golf: Its Champions and Its Championships.* 3d ed., rev. New York: Alfred A. Knopf, 1975, Revised, p. 14.
6. Quoted in Thomas P. Stewart, ed., *A Tribute to Golf: A Celebration in Art, Photography and Literature.* Harbor Springs, MI: Stewart, Hunter and Associates, 1990, p. 78.
7. Quoted in William H. Davis, *The World's Best Golf.* New York: Golf Digest/Tennis, and Pocket Books, 1991, p. 6.
8. Quoted in James A. Frank, *The Golfer's Companion.* Toronto, Ontario: Key Porter Books, 1992, p. 15.
9. David Stirk, *Golf: The History of an Obsession.* Oxford, England: Phaidon Press, 1987, p. 73.
10. Quoted in Ken Janke, *Golf Is A Funny Game . . . But It Wasn't Meant to Be.* Ann Arbor, MI: Momentum Books, 1992, p. 5.
11. Quoted in Cliff Schrock, *The Golfer's Sourcebook.* Los Angeles: Lowell House, 1998, p. 19.
12. Wind, *The Story of American Golf,* p. 9.
13. George Peper, ed., *Golf in America: The First One Hundred Years.* New York: Harry N. Abrams, 1988, pp. 14, 16.
14. Quoted in *Back Then: A Pictorial History of American Golf.* Minocqua, WI: NorthWord Press, 1990, p. 19.

15. Wind, *The Story of American Golf,* p. 30.
16. Quoted in Marcia Chambers, *The Unplayable Lie: The Untold Story of Women and Discrimination in American Golf.* New York: Pocket Books, 1995, p. 12.
17. Quoted in Rhonda Glenn, *The Illustrated History of Women's Golf.* Dallas, TX.: Taylor, 1991, p. 6.

Chapter 2: The Basics of the Game

18. Quoted in William C. Kroen, *The Why Book of Golf: 200 Practical Tips and Fascinating Facts about Golf Traditions, Rules and Etiquette.* Los Angeles: Price Stern Sloan, 1992, p. 3.
19. Quoted in Stewart, *A Tribute to Golf,* p. 20.
20. Quoted in Canfield et al., *Chicken Soup for the Golfer's Soul,* p. 81.
21. Quoted in Editors of *Golf Magazine, Golf Magazine's Encyclopedia of Golf: The Complete Reference,* 2d ed. New York: HarperCollins, 1993, p. 118.
22. Quoted in Schrock, *The Golfer's Sourcebook,* p. 40.
23. Quoted in Al Barkow, David Barrett, and Ken Janke, *Wit and Wisdom of Golf: Insightful Truths and Bad Lies.* Lincolnwood, IL: Publications International, 1998, p. 33.
24. Quoted in Schrock, *The Golfer's Sourcebook,* p. 13.
25. John Allan May, *The Complete Book of Golf: A Guide to Equipment, Techniques, and Courses.* New York: W. H. Smith, 1991, p. 11.
26. Johnny Miller and Dale Shankland, *Pure Golf.* Garden City, NY: Doubleday, 1976, p. 149.
27. Miller and Shankland, *Pure Golf,* pp. 147–48.
28. Quoted in Stirk, *Golf,* p. 24.
29. Quoted in Canfield et al., *Chicken Soup for the Golfer's Soul,* p. 109.
30. Quoted in Schrock, *The Golfer's Sourcebook,* p. 287.
31. Bob Rotella and Bob Cullen, *Golf Is Not a Game of Perfect.* New York: Simon and Schuster, 1995, p. 114.
32. Rotella and Cullen, *Golf Is Not a Game of Perfect,* p. 120.
33. Quoted in Alec Morrison, ed., *The Impossible Art of Golf: An Anthology of Golf Writing.* Oxford, England: Oxford University Press, 1995, p. 10.

Chapter 3: Evolving Through the Centuries

34. Quoted in Morrison, *The Impossible Art of Golf,* p. 20.
35. Editors of *Golf Magazine, Golf Magazine's Encyclopedia of Golf,* pp. 5–6.
36. Frank, *The Golfer's Companion,* p. 23.
37. Wind, *The Story of American Golf,* p. 42.
38. Frank, *The Golfer's Companion,* p. 24.
39. Peper, *Golf in America,* p. 184.
40. Quoted in *Sports Illustrated,* "Great

Leaps Forward," February 28, 2000, p. G17.

41. Quoted in "Great Leaps Forward," p. G17.

42. Scott Kramer, "State of the Game: Technology," *Golf Magazine*, October 1999, p. 144.

43. Editors of *Golf Magazine*, *Golf Magazine's Encyclopedia of Golf*, p. 345.

44. Peper, *Golf in America*, p. 98.

45. Quoted in David Barrett, "The Way Things Were," *Golf Magazine*, November 1997, p. 102.

46. Stirk, *Golf*, p. 128.

47. Quoted in Peper, *Golf in America*, p. 99.

48. Quoted in Pat Ward-Thomas, ed., *The World Atlas of Golf*. New York: Gallery Books, 1986, p. 33.

49. Robert R. McCord, *Golf: An Album of Its History*. Short Hills, NJ: Buford Books, 1998, p. 39.

Chapter 4: Golf's Greatest Champions

50. Quoted in David Joy, *St. Andrews and The Open Championship*. Chelsea, MI: Sleeping Bear Press, 1999, p. 30.

51. Quoted in Joy, *St. Andrews and The Open Championship*, p. 22.

52. Quoted in Wind, *The Story of American Golf*, p. 82.

53. Quoted in Evans, *Encyclopaedia of Golf*, p. 158.

54. Al Barkow, *The History of the PGA Tour*. New York: Doubleday, 1989, p. 16.

55. Quoted in Barkow, *The History of the PGA Tour*, p. 3.

56. Quoted in Peper, *Golf in America*, p. 53.

57. Quoted in Robert LaMarche, ed., *1999 Masters Journal*. Augusta, GA: Augusta National Golf Club, 1999, p. 120.

58. Quoted in Lawrence Sheehan, *A Passion for Golf: Treasures and Traditions of the Game*. New York: Clarkson Potter, 1994, p. 87.

59. Quoted in Wind, *The Story of American Golf*, p. 356.

60. Quoted in May, *The Complete Book of Golf*, p. 163.

61. Barkow, *The History of the PGA Tour*, p. 128.

62. Quoted in Janke, *Golf Is a Funny Game*, p. 112.

63. Quoted in LaMarche, *1999 Masters Journal*, p. 21.

64. Quoted in Rick Reilly, "Top Cat," *Sports Illustrated*, October 28, 1996, p. 46.

65. Quoted in Glenn, *The Illustrated History of Women's Golf*, p. 57.

66. Quoted in Robert McCord, *The Golf Book of Days: Fascinating Golf Facts and Stories for Every Day of the Year*. New York: Birch Lane Press, 1995, p. 183.

67. Quoted in Wind, *The Story of American Golf*, p. 355.

68. Quoted in Jerry Potter, "Tour Co-Founder

Finally Gets Due," *USA Today,* January 13, 2000, p. 3C.

69. Morrison, *The Impossible Art of Golf,* p. 113.

70. Glenn, *The Illustrated History of Women's Golf,* p. 281.

Chapter 5: The Changing Face of Golf

71. Quoted in Rick Reilly, "Strokes of Genius," *Sports Illustrated,* April 21, 1997, p. 35.

72. Quoted in Pete McDaniel, "The Trailblazer." *Golf Digest,* April 2000, p. 164.

73. John Pinner, *The History of Golf.* New York: Gallery Books, 1988, p. 11.

74. Chambers, *The Unplayable Lie,* p. 4.

75. Quoted in *Black Enterprise,* "Teeing off: History of Blacks in Golf," September 1994, p. 69.

76. Quoted in Calvin H. Sinnette, *Forbidden Fairways: African Americans and the Game of Golf.* Chelsea, MI: Sleeping Bear Press, 1998, p. 54.

77. Sinnette, *Forbidden Fairways,* p. 133.

78. Quoted in Glenn, *The Illustrated History of Women's Golf,* p. 218.

79. Quoted in Don Walker, "Woods En Route to Conquer Even More Worlds," *Milwaukee Journal Sentinel,* February 9, 2000, p. C2.

80. Quoted in Len Shapiro, "State of the Game: Access," *Golf Magazine,* June, 1998, p. 131.

81. Quoted in Thomas Bonk, "Uncommon Liaw," *Golf Magazine,* June 1999, p. 66.

82. Wind, *The Story of American Golf,* p. 37.

83. Chambers, *The Unplayable Lie,* p. 3.

84. Guido P. Cribari, "Golfers with Disabilities Are on Course," *WE Magazine,* July/August 1998, p. 53.

85. Quoted in Alan Shipnuck, "Next Case," *Sports Illustrated,* January 31, 2000, p. G6.

86. Author interviewed Greg Jones by telephone from Franklin, WI, March 18, 2000.

87. Quoted in Tim Rosaforte, *Tiger Woods: The Makings of a Champion.* New York: St. Martin's Press, 1997, p. 104.

Epilogue: Twenty-First-Century Golf

88. Stewart, *A Tribute to Golf,* p. 27.

89. Quoted in Noel Neff, ed., *The Andersen Consulting World Championship of Golf.* Clearwater, FL: International Sports Marketing Group, 1995, p. 195.

90. Stewart, *A Tribute to Golf,* p. 27.

91. Quoted in Schrock, *The Golfer's Sourcebook,* p. 137.

92. Sean Nolan, "Spruce up Your Golf Game Online," *Access,* April 30, 2000, p. 18.

93. Wind, *The Story of American Golf,* p. 5.

Glossary

address: The posture a golfer assumes before swinging the club.

away: The golfer who is the farthest from the hole among those playing.

ball marker: A small round object, sometimes a coin, used to mark balls on the green.

birdie: A score on a hole that is one stroke less than par.

bogey: A score on a hole that is one stroke more than par; a double bogey is two over par, and so forth.

bunker: A depression in the fairway or near the greens, usually filled with sand, designed to penalize golfers who hit into them; also called a trap.

caddie: The person who carries a golfer's clubs and provides advice on club selection and shot strategy.

carry: The distance a ball flies when it is struck.

chip shot: A short approach shot from near the green.

clubhead: The part of the club that strikes the ball.

dimples: The round indentations on a golf ball's cover, which help the ball fly straight when it is hit.

dogleg: A right-hand or left-hand bend in a fairway.

divot: A chunk of grass and earth torn out of the ground by a player swinging a club.

double eagle: A score on a hole that is three strokes less than par; called an albatross in Europe.

drive: The golfer's first shot on each hole, also called a tee shot.

eagle: A score on a hole that is two strokes less than par.

face: The surface on the clubhead that comes in contact with the ball.

fairway: The well-tended grass area that is the intended route from the tee to the green.

flagstick: A pole with a flag that is inserted into the hole to indicate its position.

fore: The warning a player yells after hitting an errant shot to alert other golfers; it is believed this term is derived from the warning to infantry soldiers before the British fired artillery.

fringe: Short-cut grass surrounding the green.

front nine: The first nine holes in a round of golf; the last nine are the back nine.

grand slam: Refers to winning, in one year, all four of the men's major golf champions; first used to describe Bobby Jones's four victories in 1930 in the U.S. Amateur, U.S. Open, British Amateur, and British Open, the four major tournaments of his era.

green: Extremely short cut grass on which the player putts to get the ball in the hole.

green fee: The cost of a round of golf.

grip: The way a golfer holds the club; also the part of the club shaft the player holds.

hazard: Bunkers, bodies of water, trees, and other obstacles (such as boulders) placed strategically on a course to make it more challenging.

hole: The cavity (4.25 inches wide and 4 inches deep) cut out of the green; also called the cup.

hole in one: A tee shot that lands in the cup; also called an ace.

hook: A mishit shot that curves to the left of the target for a right-hand golfer and to the right for a left-hand golfer.

lie: The position of a ball on the ground while it is in play.

links: A golf course.

loft: The angle of the face of the club.

match play: A tournament decided by the golfer who wins the most individual holes by recording the lowest score on those holes in a round.

major: There are four major championships in men's professional golf: the British Open, the Masters, the Professional Golfers Association Tournament, and the U. S. Open.

medal play: A tournament decided by the number of strokes players take; also called a stroke play.

open: A tournament in which both amateurs and professionals compete.

par: The score a good player should make on a particular hole—3, 4, or 5 depending on its rating—or the total number of strokes required to play the entire course.

penalty stroke: A stroke added to a player's score for violating the rules, such as losing a ball.

pot bunker: A small but deep sand trap.

purse: The total amount of money awarded to all golfers entered in a professional tournament.

putt: One stroke taken on the green.

rough: Taller grass bordering the fairway and surrounding the green.

shaft: The handle of the golf club.

slice: A shot in which the ball curves to the right of the target for a right-handed golfer or to the left for a left-handed golfer.

stance: The position of a golfer's feet prior to addressing the ball.

tee: The marked-off area in which golfers stand to make their first shot on each hole; also called the tee box.

Chronology

1457
On March 6, King James II bans golf in Scotland because it interferes with archery practice.

1608
Golf is played for the first time in England, on London's Blackheath Common.

1743
The Goff by Thomas Mathison, the first publication strictly about golf, is printed on May 14.

1744
The Gentlemen Golfers of Edinburgh, later renamed the Honourable Company of Edinburgh Golfers, become the first organized golf club and set down golf's first rules.

1754
The Society of St. Andrews Golfers, later to become the Royal and Ancient Golf Club of St. Andrews, is founded in Scotland May 12.

1764
St. Andrews reconfigures its course to establish eighteen as the standard number of holes.

1772
Dr. Benjamin Rush gives golf its first mention in an American publication, a pamphlet on the importance of exercise for good health.

1829
The Royal Calcutta Club in India is the first golf club founded outside of Great Britain.

1834
English King William IV awards St. Andrews its designation of "Royal and Ancient."

1845
The Reverend James Paterson of Dundee, Scotland, is credited with making the first gutta-percha ball.

1856
The first golf course in Europe opens at Pau, France.

1860
Willie Park Sr. wins the first British Open.

1861
"Old Tom" Morris wins the first of his four British Opens; his son, "Young Tom" Morris, will also win four Opens.

1867
The St. Andrews Ladies' Club is founded, the world's first for women.

1888

On February 22, John Reid and a friend, John B. Upham, play golf in a cow pasture near his home in Yonkers, New York, bringing the game of golf to America for good; on November 14 Reid and five other golfers found the St. Andrew's Golf Club, the nation's oldest continuously operating club.

1894

Representatives of five country clubs found the U.S. Golf Association (USGA).

1895

The USGA holds the first U.S. Amateur, U.S. Women's Amateur, and U.S. Open.

1896

John Shippen is the first non-Caucasian to enter a major tournament, finishing fifth in the U.S. Open. He was part African American and part Shinnecock Indian.

1898

Coburn Haskell patents the rubber-cored ball.

1913

Francis Ouimet gives credibility to American golf by beating two top English players, Harry Vardon and Ted Ray, to win the U.S. Open.

1916

The Professional Golfers Association of America (PGA) is founded April 10; in October Jim Barnes wins the first PGA Championship.

1925

The USGA approves steel shafts; The Royal and Ancient Golf Club of St. Andrews follows suit in 1931.

1927

The United States wins the first Ryder Cup Match at Worcester, Massachusetts.

1930

Bobby Jones win the U.S. Open, British Open and the U.S. and British amateur titles; he retires after his grand slam of major titles.

1938

Golf is broadcast for the first time on July 15 when the British Broadcasting Corporation televises a match near London, England.

1945

Byron Nelson wins eleven consecutive PGA Tournaments.

1947

Golf appears on American television when the final round of the 1947 U.S. Open is telecast.

1950

The Ladies Professional Golf Association (LPGA) is formed and in January holds its first tournament.

1961

The PGA revokes its policy barring non-Caucasians.

1971

On February 5, astronaut Alan Shepard Jr. hits a golf ball on the moon during the Apollo 14 space mission.

1975

On April 10, Lee Elder becomes the first

African American to play in the Masters.

1977

Nancy Lopez debuts on the LPGA tour.

1996

After winning a record third consecutive U.S. Amateur title, Tiger Woods turns professional and wins two of eight PGA tournaments.

1997

On April 20, Woods becomes the first African American to win the Masters.

For Further Reading

Dave Anderson, *The Story of Golf*. New York: William Morrow, 1998. A history of the game for the younger reader by this veteran sportswriter.

Back Then: A Pictorial History of American Golf. Minocqua, WI: NorthWord Press, 1990. Old photographs and stories from publications of that era provide an interesting look at golf in its first few decades in America.

Rhonda Glenn, *The Illustrated History of Women's Golf*. Dallas, TX: Taylor, 1991. Glenn, a fine amateur golfer and former television analyst, has written an interesting study of the role women have played in golf.

Ken Janke, *Golf Is A Funny Game . . . But It Wasn't Meant to Be*. Ann Arbor, MI: Momentum Books, 1992. A collection of amusing, entertaining, and sometimes educational quotes, anecdotes, and historical facts about golf.

William C. Kroen, *The Why Book of Golf: 200 Practical Tips and Fascinating Facts About Golf Traditions, Rules and Etiquette*. Los Angeles: Price Stern Sloan, 1992. A good book for someone new to golf, it provides simple explanations of the game's history, its terms, and how to play.

Robert R. McCord, *Golf: An Album of Its History*. Short Hills, NJ: Buford Books, 1998. Interesting pictures and accompanying text blocks that explain, in a somewhat disjointed fashion, the history of golf.

John Pinner, *The History of Golf*. New York: Gallery Books, 1988. A well-researched, readable book about golf's history.

Lawrence Sheehan, *A Passion for Golf: Treasures and Traditions of the Game*. New York: Clarkson Potter, 1994. The many pictures and full-color illustrations provide a unique look at golf's past.

Calvin H. Sinnette, *Forbidden Fairways: African Americans and the Game of Golf*. Chelsea, MI: Sleeping Bear Press, 1998. A well-researched, thought-provoking account of the problems racism caused for both professional and amateur African American golfers.

Michael V. Uschan, *Tiger Woods*. San Diego: Lucent Books, 1999. A readable, interesting biography of the young golfer who may be the greatest ever to play the game.

Herbert Warren Wind, *The Story of American Golf: Its Champions and Its Championships*. 3d ed., rev. New York: Alfred A. Knopf, 1975. Perhaps the best history of American golf ever written, filled with interesting details the author, a golf writer for more than a half century, collected firsthand.

Works Consulted

Books

Al Barkow, *The History of the PGA Tour.* New York: Doubleday, 1989. A fact-filled account of professional golf in America.

Al Barkow, David Barrett, and Ken Janke, *Wit and Wisdom of Golf: Insightful Truths and Bad Lies.* Lincolnwood, IL: Publications International, 1998. A collection of amusing quotes, anecdotes, and bits of history about golf.

Schuyler Bishop, ed., *A Passion for Golf: The Best of Golf Writing.* New York: St. Martin's Press, 1998. The author has included some of the most interesting articles and pieces of fiction ever penned about golf or golfers.

Vincent Borremans, *Golf: The Game and Its Champions.* New York: Universe Publishing, 1998. A solid look at some of the greatest players in golf's long history.

Sheperd Campbell and Peter Landau, *Presidential Lies: The Illustrated History of White House Golf.* New York: Macmillan, 1996. Pictures and text provide an amusing look at the love affair U.S. presidents have had with golf, from William Taft to Bill Clinton.

Jack Canfield et al., *Chicken Soup for the Golfer's Soul: 101 Stories of Insight, Inspiration and Laughter on the Links.* Deerfield Beach, FL: Health Communications, 1999. As he has done in other books in this series, the author has collected dramatic, uplifting personal stories on a particular topic, this one focusing on golf.

Marcia Chambers, *The Unplayable Lie: The Untold Story of Women and Discrimination in American Golf.* New York: Pocket Books, 1995. Chambers, a golfer and legal expert, outlines the discrimination women golfers have had to deal with from the game's earliest days.

Frank Coffey, *Why Do They Call It A Birdie?: 1,001 Fascinating Facts About Golf.* Secaucus, NJ: Birth Lane Press, 1996. Short pieces that answer a variety of questions about golf in an insightful, entertaining way.

Henry Cotton, *A History of Golf Illustrated.* New York: B. Lippincott, 1975. A British Open champion from the 1920s who became a journalist, Cotton gives a detailed account of golf's history; the book focuses on British golf.

William H. Davis, *The World's Best Golf.* New York: Golf Digest/Tennis, and Pocket Books, 1991. The author provides commentary on golf course architecture and discusses some of the world's best courses; pictures of the courses discussed are a treat.

Webster Evans, *Encyclopaedia of Golf.* New York: St. Martin's Press, 1974. Information about golf in an encyclopedia format with some fifteen hundred entries.

James A. Frank, *The Golfer's Companion.* Toronto, Ontario: Key Porter Books, 1992. A well-documented book that discusses the history of the sport, evolution of golf equipment, and the game's greatest players.

Editors of *Golf Magazine, Golf Magazine's Encyclopedia of Golf: The Complete Reference,* 2d ed. New York: HarperCollins, 1993. This encyclopedia provides exhaustive detail on a wide variety of golf topics, including how to play.

Robert T. Jones Jr. and O. B. Keeler, *Down the Fairway.* 1927. Reprint, New York: Ailsa, 1985. First published in 1927. An autobiography that covers only part of Jones's fascinating life.

David Joy, *St. Andrews and The Open Championship.* Chelsea, MI: Sleeping Bear Press, 1999. This St. Andrews native recounts the British Opens contested on the fabled course. Pictures of St. Andrews, from past to present, are its main strength.

Robert LaMarche, ed., *1999 Masters Journal.* Augusta, GA: Augusta National Golf Club, 1999. This is the annual program published and sold at the Masters Tournament.

John Allan May, *The Complete Book of Golf: A Guide to Equipment, Techniques, and Courses.* New York: W. H. Smith, 1991. A great source of information for someone who wants to learn about the topics discussed.

Robert N. McCord, *The Golf Book of Days: Fascinating Golf Facts and Stories for Every Day of the Year.* New York: Birch Lane Press, 1995. A different topic for each day, including biographical information on golfing greats and bits of history of the game.

Johnny Miller and Dale Shankland, *Pure Golf.* Garden City, NY: Doubleday, 1976. Miller, once one of the world's best golfers, explains how to play.

Alec Morrison, ed., *The Impossible Art of Golf: An Anthology of Golf Writing.* Oxford, England: Oxford University Press, 1995. Pieces of fiction, nonfiction, and poetry about golf that explain its history and why so many are fascinated with the game.

Noel Neff, ed., *The Andersen Consulting World Championship of Golf.* Clearwater, FL: International Sports Marketing

Group, 1995. A publication produced for the match play world championship; it has interesting articles on players and golf history.

Arnold Palmer, *My Game and Yours*. New York: Simon and Schuster, 1965. A partly autobiographical work that gives the reader instructions in how to play golf.

Arnold Palmer and James Dodson. *A Golfer's Life*. New York. New York: Ballantine Books, 1999. An autobiography of one of the greatest golfers in the game's history.

George Peper, ed., *Golf in America: The First One Hundred Years*. New York: Harry N. Abrams, 1988. A very interesting, well-researched look at how golf began and flourished in its first century in the United States.

The PGA Media Guide. Palm Beach Gardens, FL: A PGA Publication, 1999. The annual media guide that includes biographical material on players, statistics, history, and other data.

Tim Rosaforte, *Tiger Woods: The Makings of a Champion*. New York: St. Martin's Press, 1997. A solid biography by a veteran sports journalist.

Bob Rotella and Bob Cullen, *Golf Is Not a Game of Perfect*. New York: Simon and Schuster, 1995. Rotella, a sports psychologist, explains how he has helped various golfers improve their confidence and concentration.

Cliff Schrock, *The Golfer's Sourcebook*. Los Angeles: Lowell House, 1998. The author details golf's long history and discusses a wide variety of golf topics, including social issues such as course etiquette.

Thomas P. Stewart, ed., *A Tribute to Golf: A Celebration in Art, Photography and Literature*. Harbor Springs, MI: Stewart, Hunter and Associates, 1990. An interesting book that features great photographs and illustrations which bring golf's past alive.

David Stirk, *Golf: The History of an Obsession*. Oxford, England: Phaidon Press, 1987. The author provides a detailed history of the evolution of clubs and balls, course architecture, and other aspects of golf.

Pat Ward-Thomas, ed., *The World Atlas of Golf*. New York: Gallery Books, 1986. A review of some of the best courses each country has to offer the avid golfer.

Gary Wiren, *The PGA Manual of Golf: The Professional's Way to Play Better Golf*. New York: Macmillan, 1991. This book explains the general history of golf and includes very technical, detailed sections on topics like how to play and how to choose clubs; not recommended for the general reader.

Periodicals

David Barrett, "The Way Things Were," *Golf Magazine*, November 1997.

Black Enterprise, "Teeing off: History of Blacks in Golf," September 1994.

Thomas Bonk, "Uncommon Liaw," *Golf Magazine,* June, 1999.

Guido P. Cribari, "Golfers with Disabilities Are on Course," *WE Magazine,* July/August 1998.

Jaime Diaz, "Masters Plan," *Sports Illustrated,* April 13, 1998.

Scott Kramer, "State of the Game: Technology," *Golf Magazine,* October 1999.

Sarah McCollum, "Par for the Course," *Dog World,* April 1998.

Pete McDaniel, "The Trailblazer," *Golf Digest,* April 2000.

Sean Nolan, "Spruce up Your Golf Game Online," *Access,* April 30, 2000.

Charles B. Pierce, "The Man. Amen," *Gentleman's Quarterly,* April 1997.

Rick Reilly, "Strokes of Genius," *Sports Illustrated,* April 21, 1997.

———, "Top Cat," *Sports Illustrated,* October 28, 1996.

Len Shapiro, "State of the Game: Access," *Golf Magazine,* June 1998.

Alan Shipnuck, "Next Case," *Sports Illustrated,* January 31, 2000.

Sports Illustrated, "Great Leaps Forward," February 28, 2000.

Newspapers

Harry Blauvelt, "Nelson Rooting for Woods," *USA Today,* February 3, 2000.

Doug Ferguson, "Woods Rolls On and On." Associated Press, January 9, 2000.

Jerry Potter, "Tour Co-Founder Finally Gets Due," *USA Today,* January 13, 2000.

Don Walker, "Woods En Route to Conquer Even More Worlds," *Milwaukee Journal Sentinel*, February 9, 2000.

Index

Picture Credits

Cover photo: © Bettmann/Corbis
© AFP/Corbis, 8
Archive Photos, 13 (left), 17, 59 (top), 61
Associated Press AP, 47, 64
© Bettmann/Corbis, 14, 30, 33, 42, 46, 54, 56 (left and right), 57, 59 (bottom), 70
© Corbis, 10
Express Newspapers/8123/Archive Photos, 62
FPG International, 32, 35, 51 (right), 53, 67, 77
© FPG International 1929, 49
© FPG International—1998, 40
© Charles A. Harris/Corbis, 9, 68
Hulton Getty/Archive Photos, 19, 51 (left)
© Lane Kennedy/Corbis, 74
Library of Congress, 24
North Wind Picture Archives, 12, 21
Prints Old and Rare, 16, 71
Reuters/Adrees Latif/Archive Photos, 72
© Reuters Newmedia Inc./Corbis, 58
© Tony Roberts/Corbis, 26, 37, 43 (top and bottom), 45, 66
© Robert B. J. Small/FPG International, 34
© Michael Simpson, 1992/FPG International, 29
© Richard Hamilton Smith/Corbis, 25
© Stock Montage, Inc., 13 (right), 23, 65

About the Author

Michael V. Uschan, who has written about golf extensively for newspapers and magazines, has authored ten other books including a biography of Tiger Woods. His previous works for Lucent include *Male Olympic Champions, America's Founders,* and *The Importance of John F. Kennedy.* Mr. Uschan began his career as a writer and editor with United Press International, a wire service that provides stories to newspapers, radio, and television. Journalism is sometimes called "history in a hurry," and Mr. Uschan considers writing history books a natural extension of skills he developed in his many years as a working journalist. He and his wife, Barbara, live in the Milwaukee suburb of Franklin, Wisconsin.